Copyright © 2022 Monty Books

All rights reserved
No part of this publication
may be reproduced, distributed,
transmitted in any form or by any means,
including photocopying, recording,
or other electronic or mechanical methods,
without the prior written permission
of the publisher, except in the case of
brief quotations embodied in critical reviews
and certain other noncommercial uses
permitted by copyright law

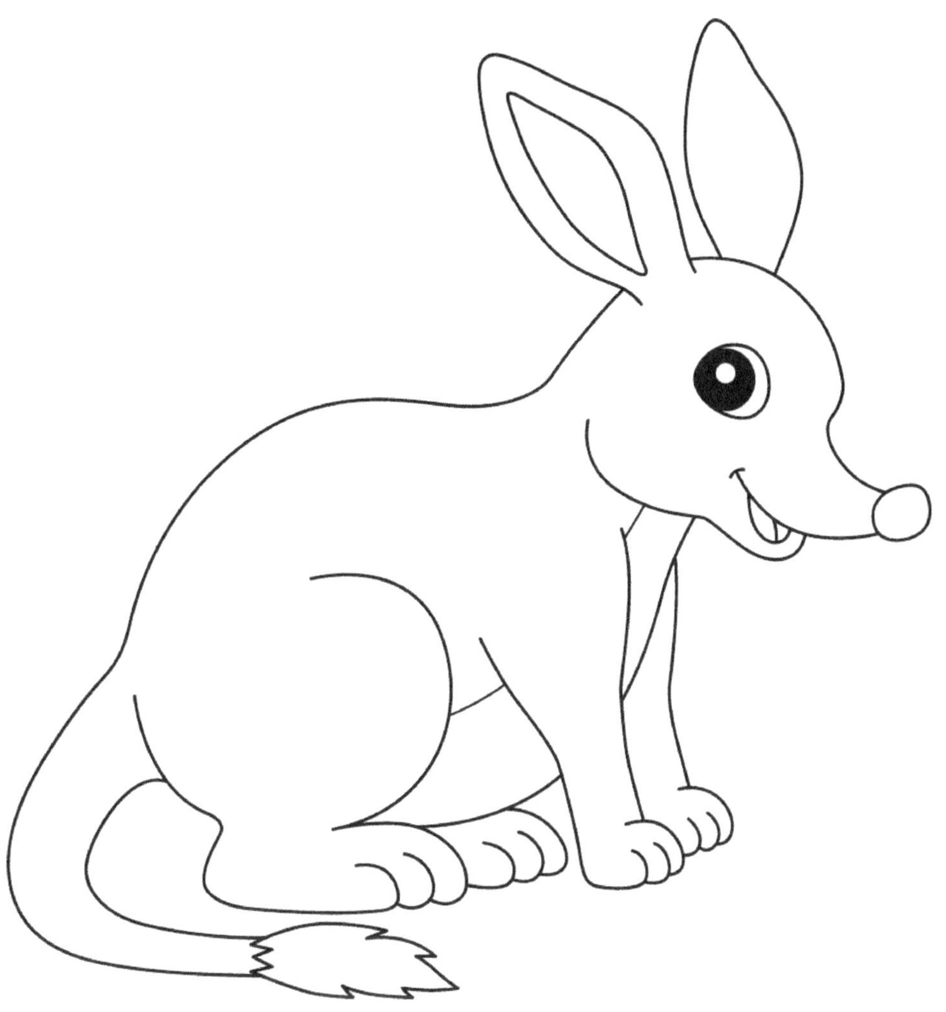

This Book Belongs To

____

____

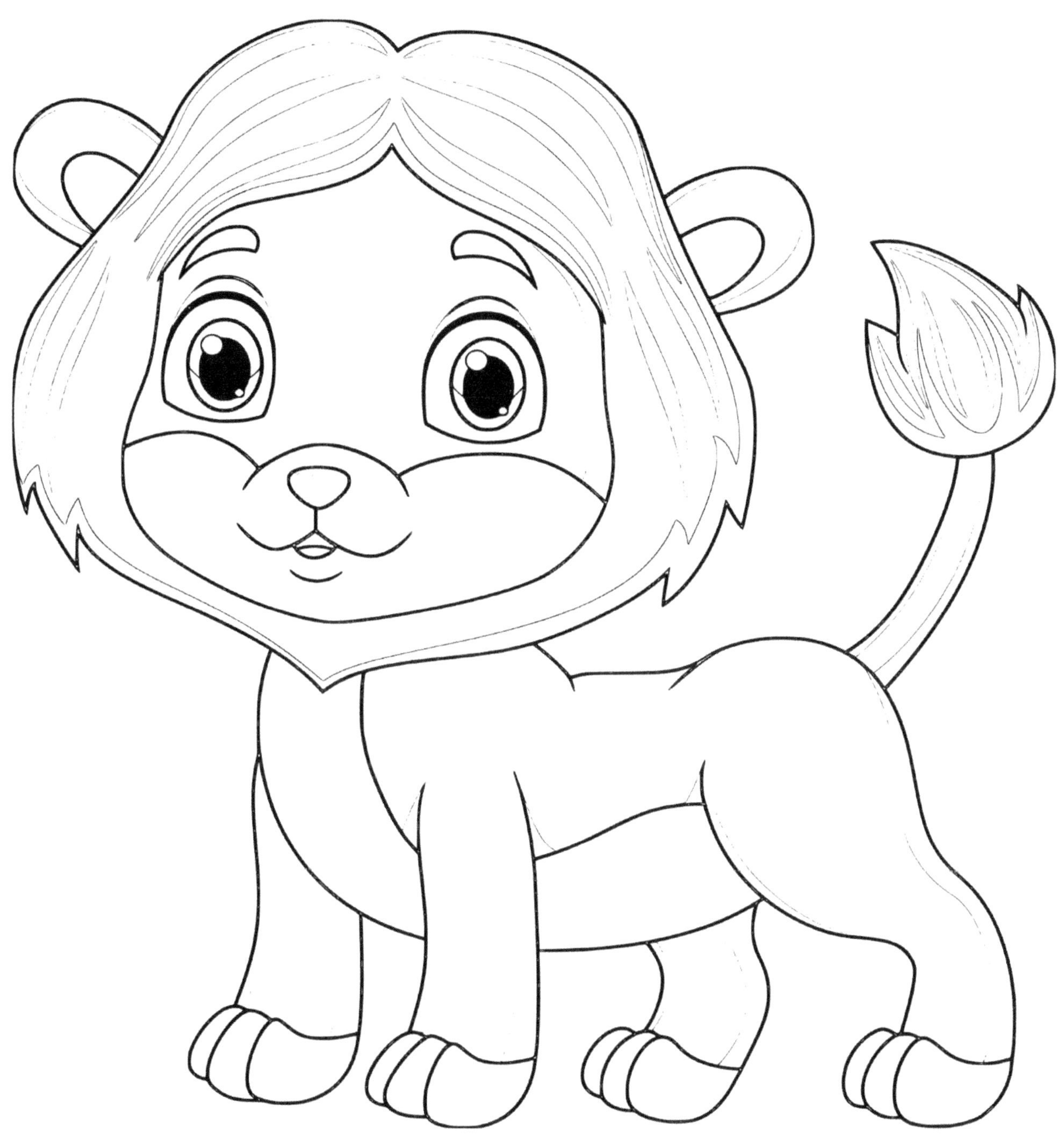

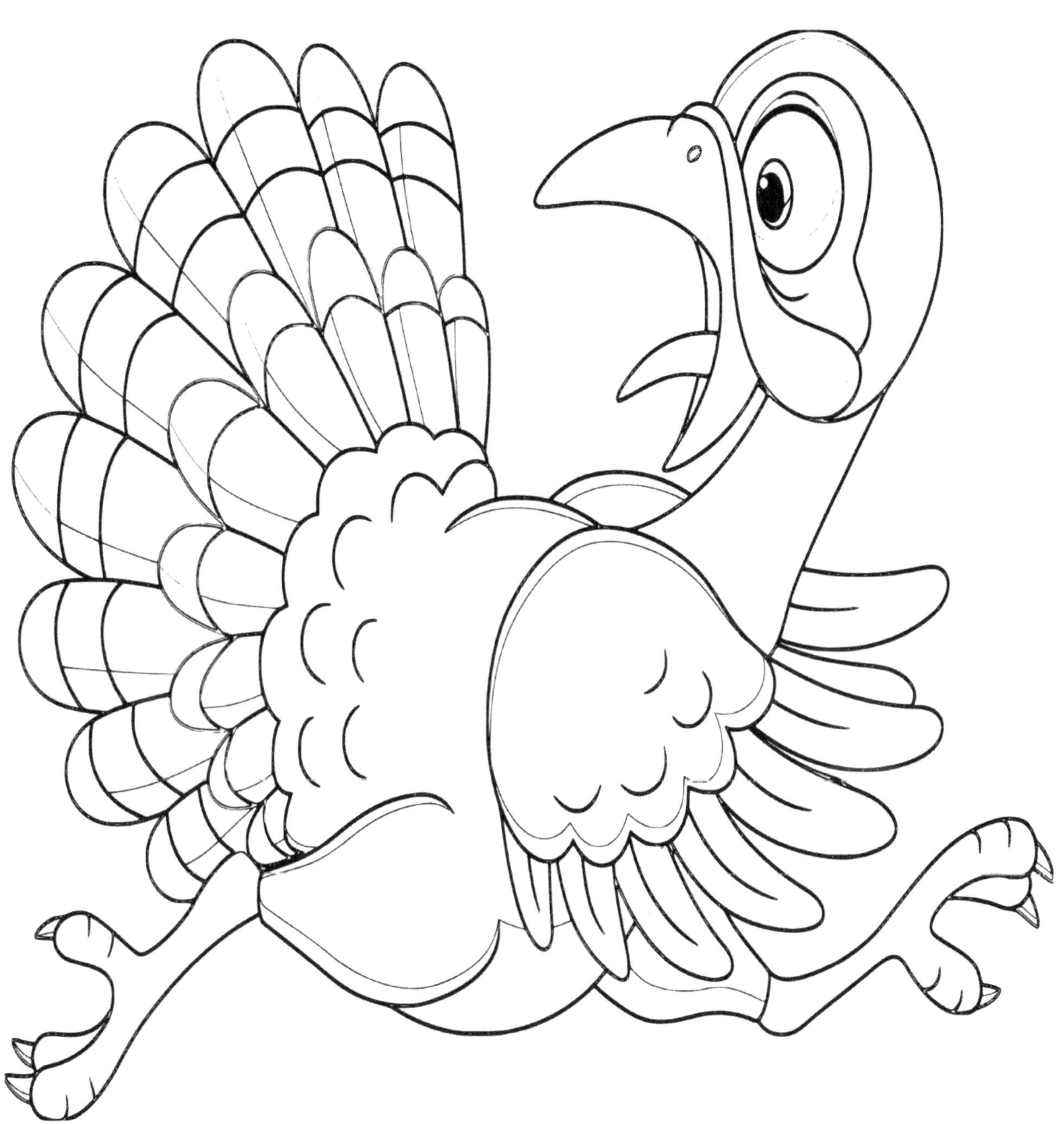

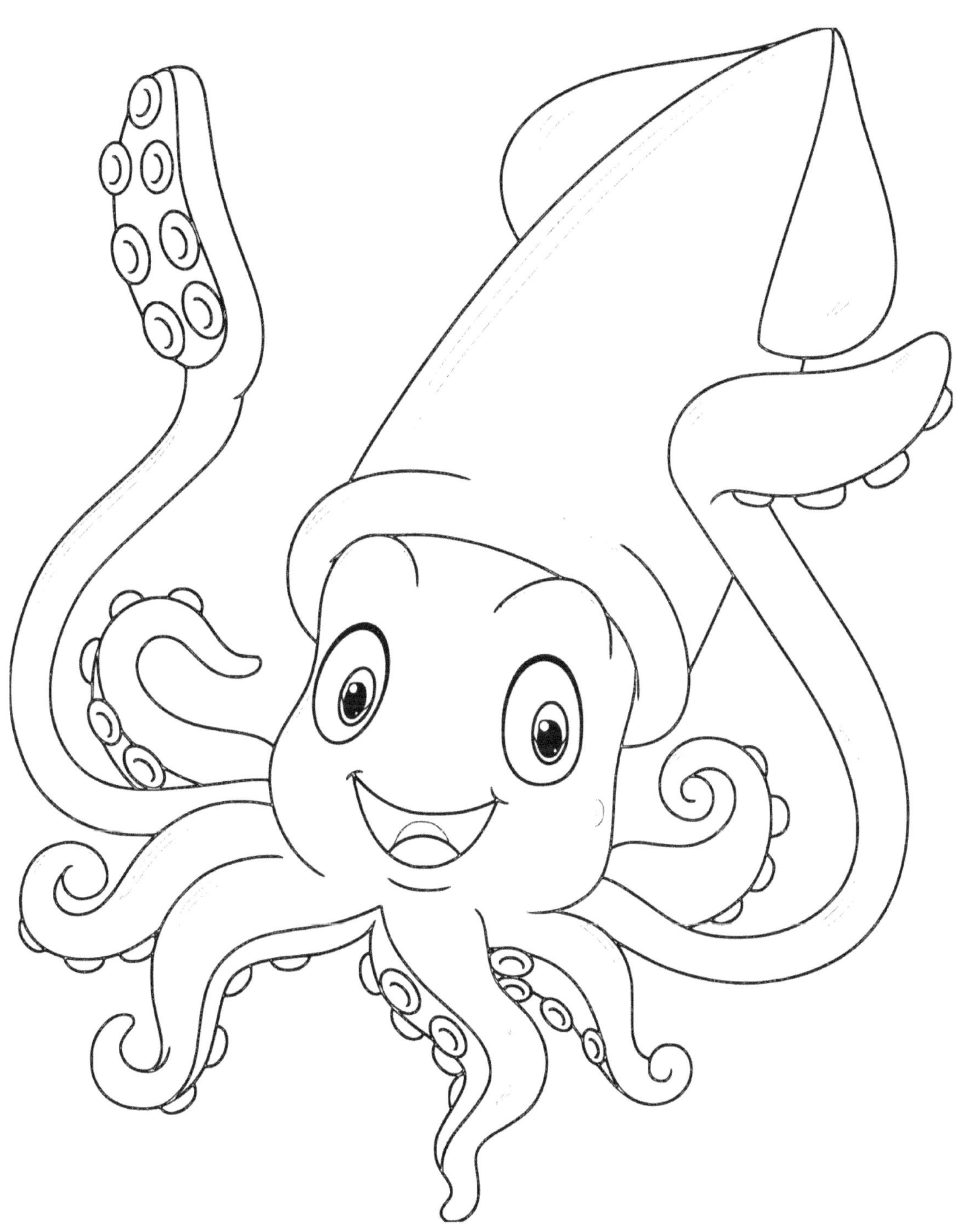

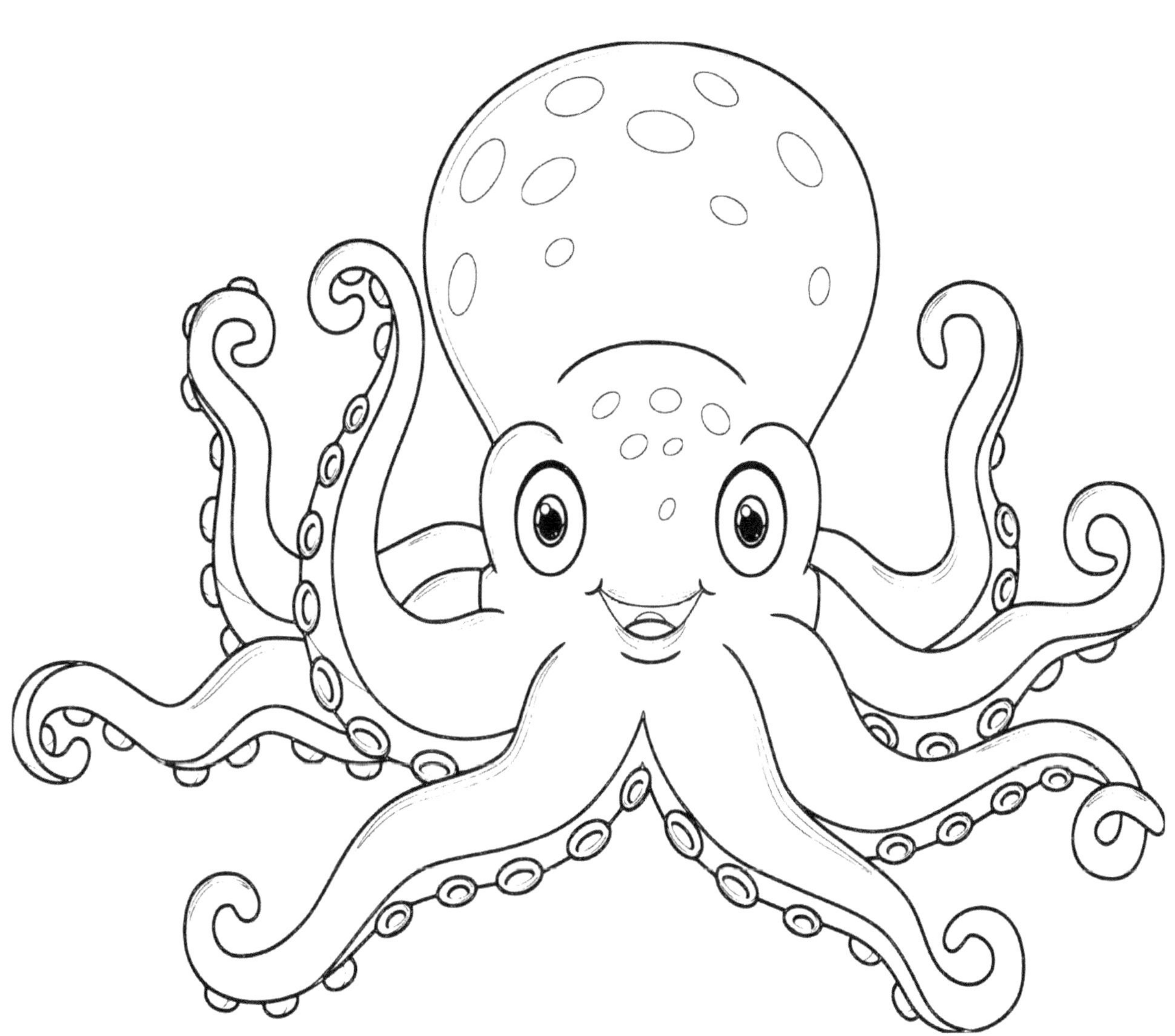

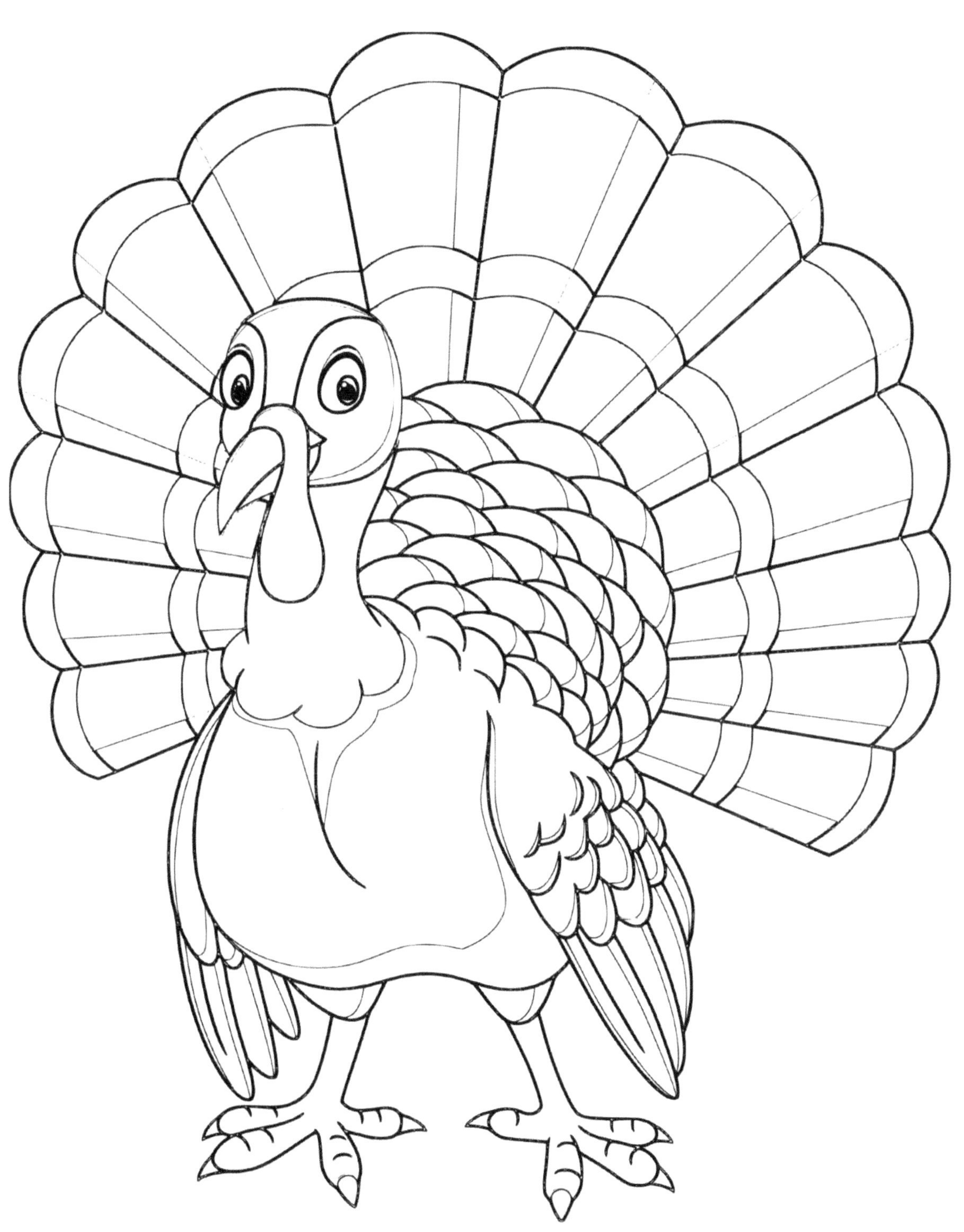

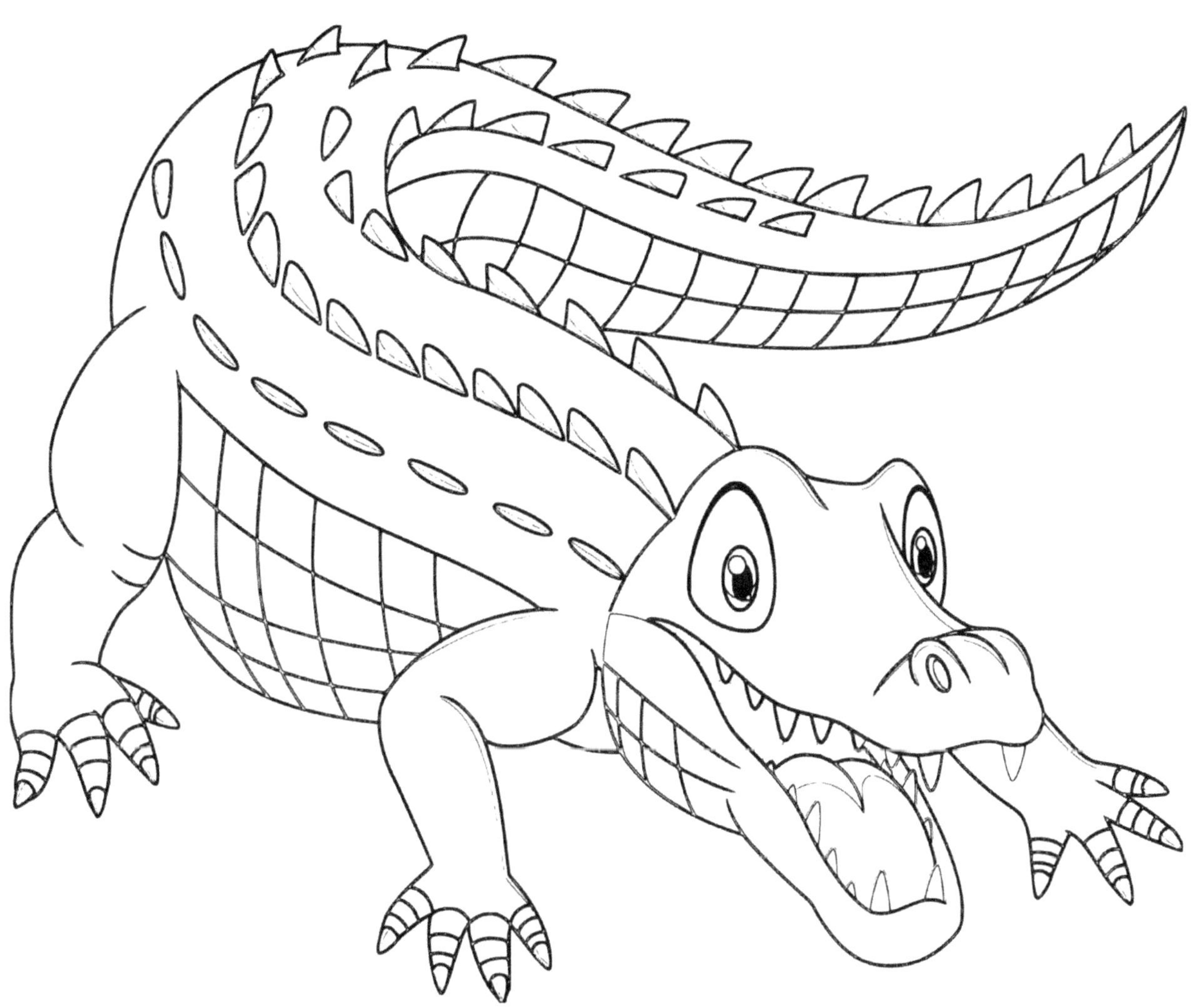

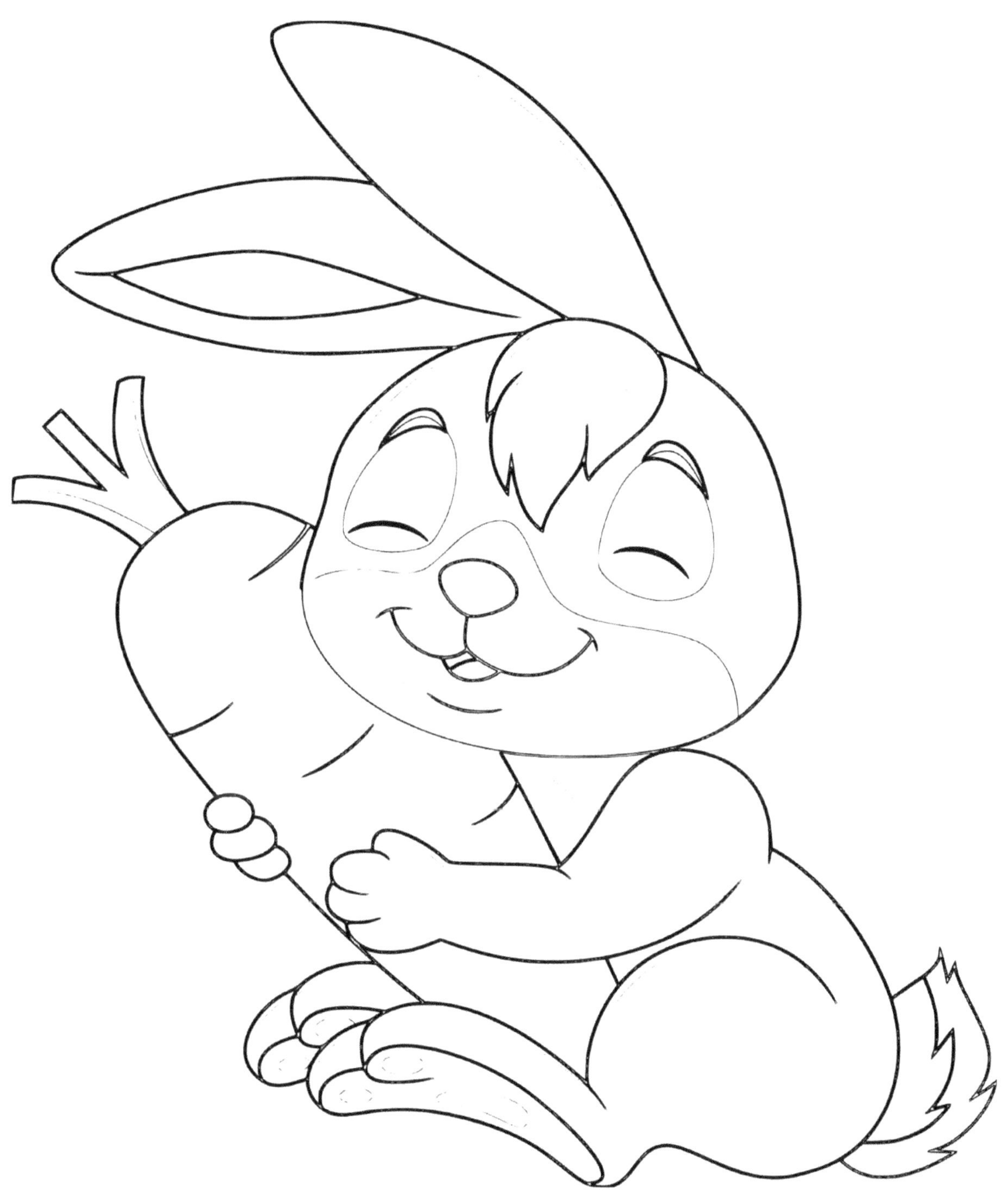

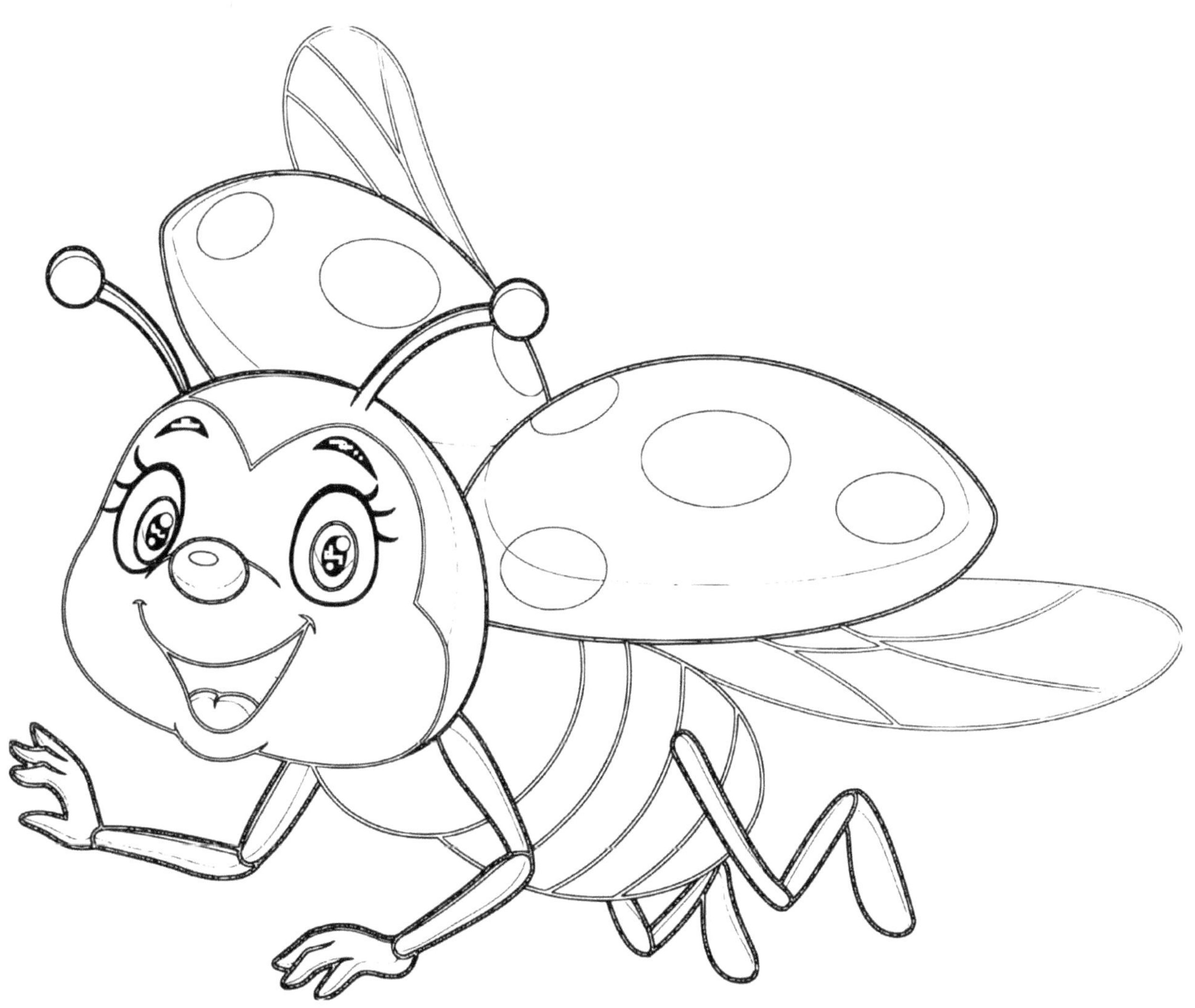

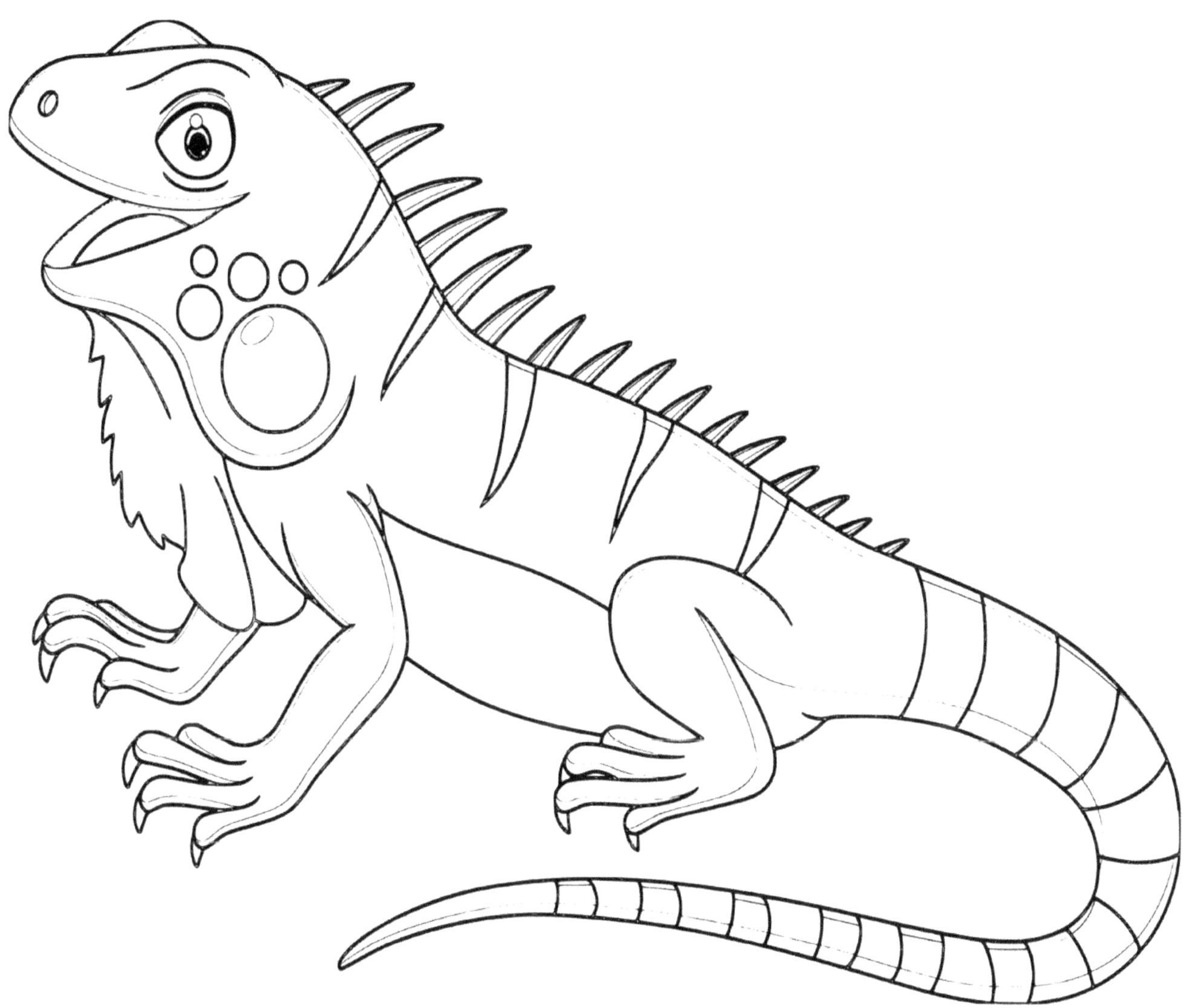

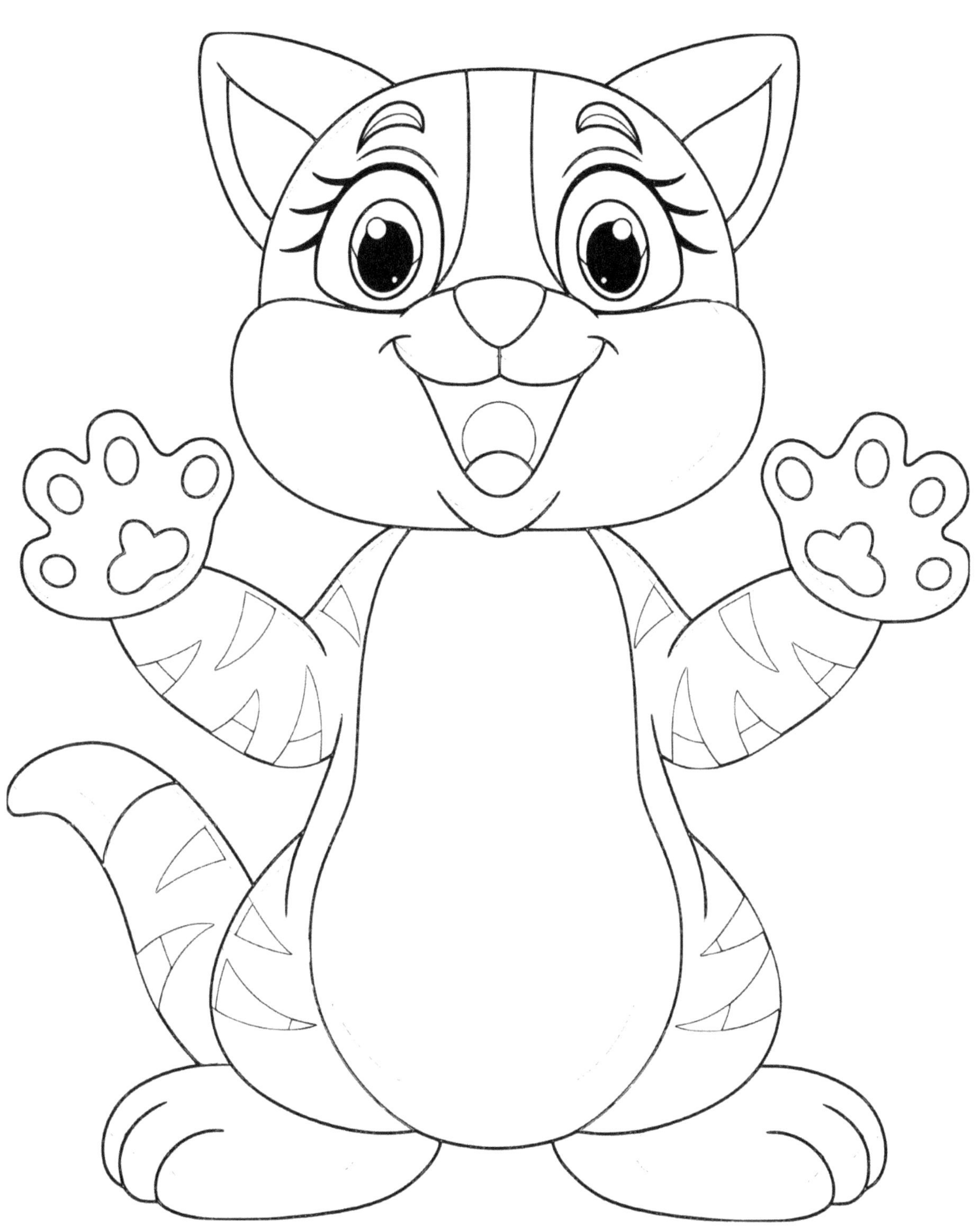

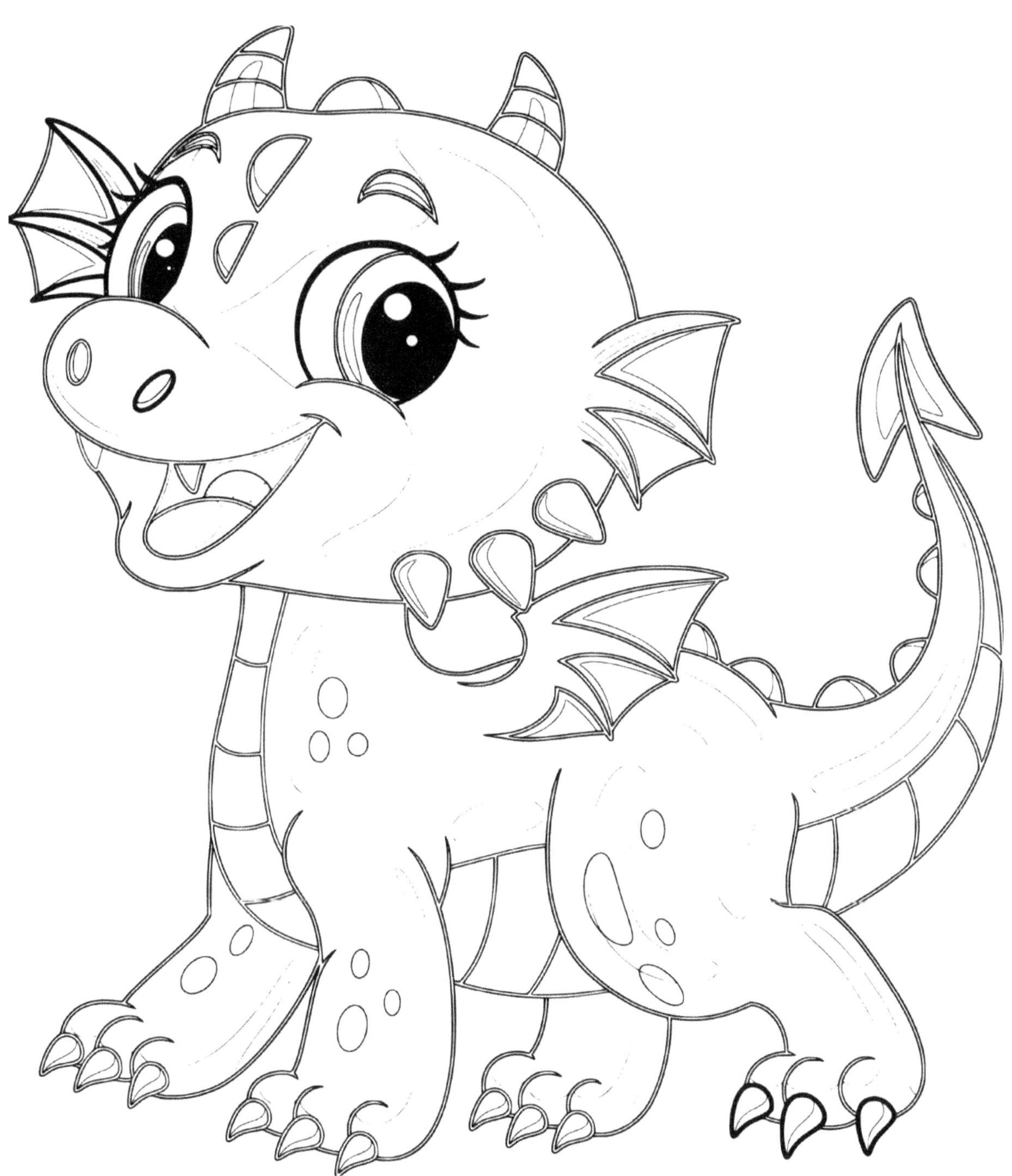

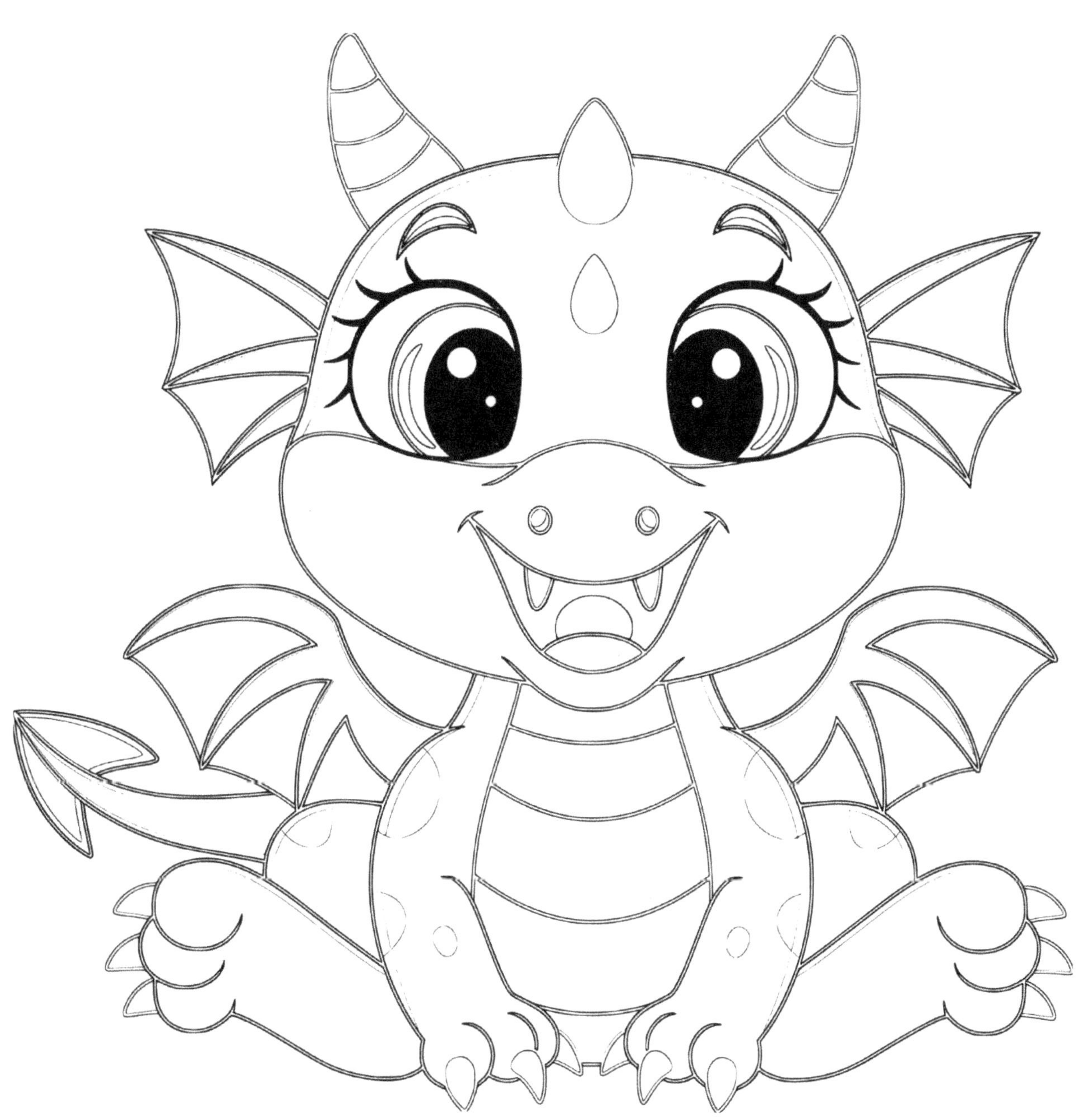

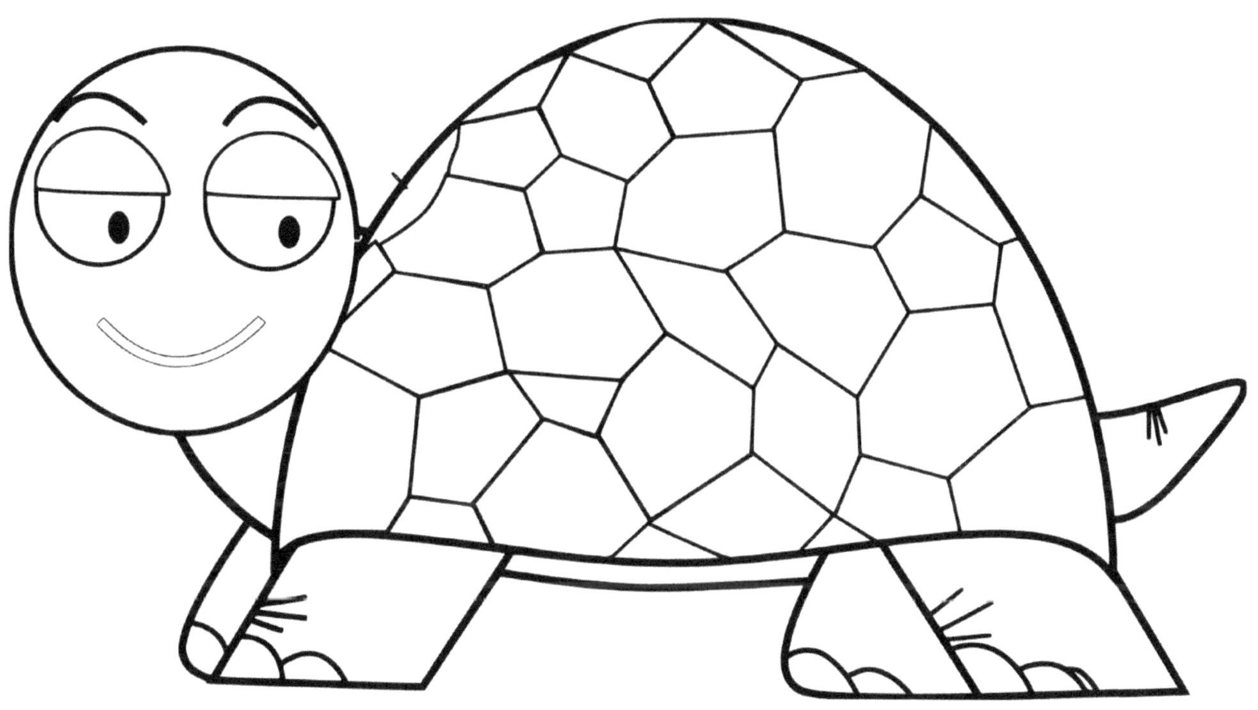

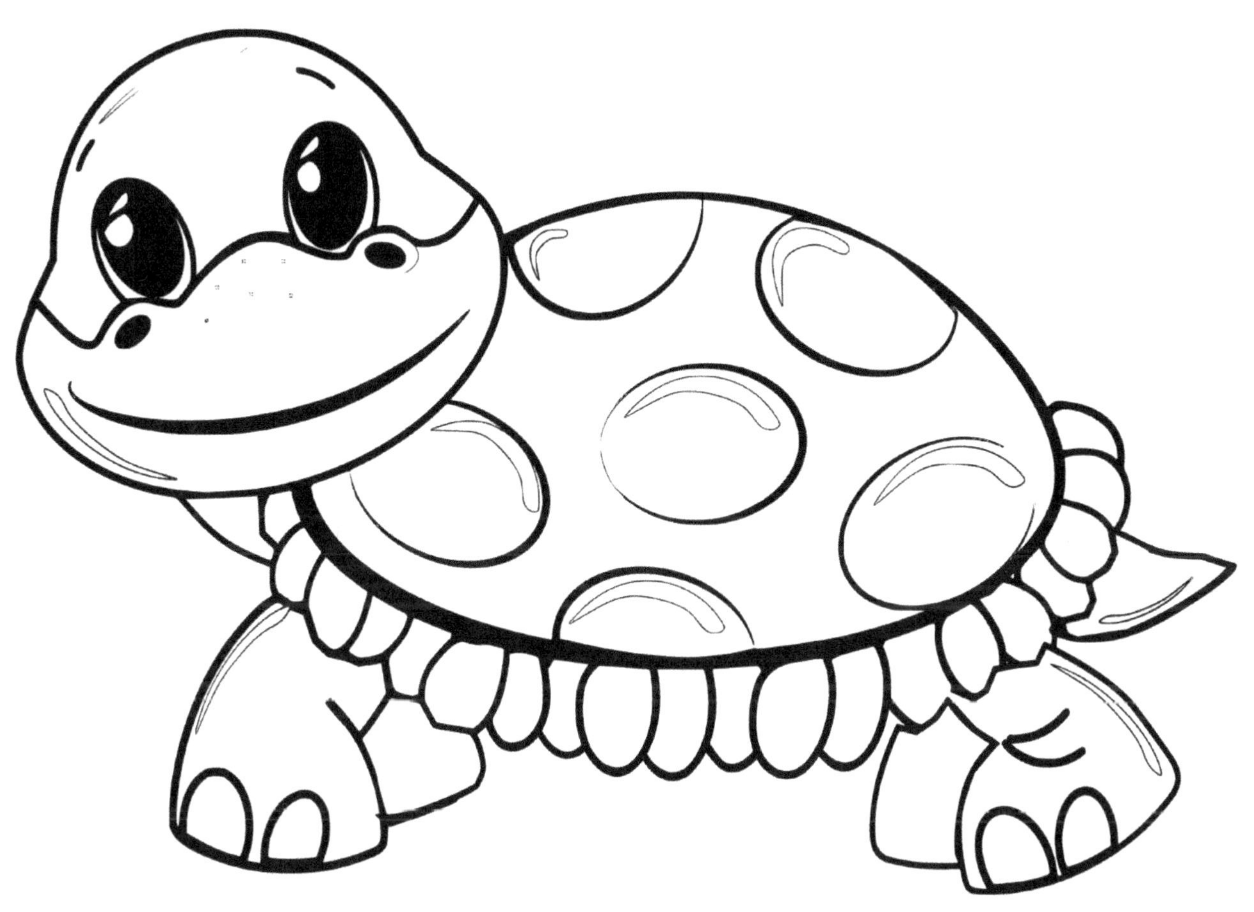

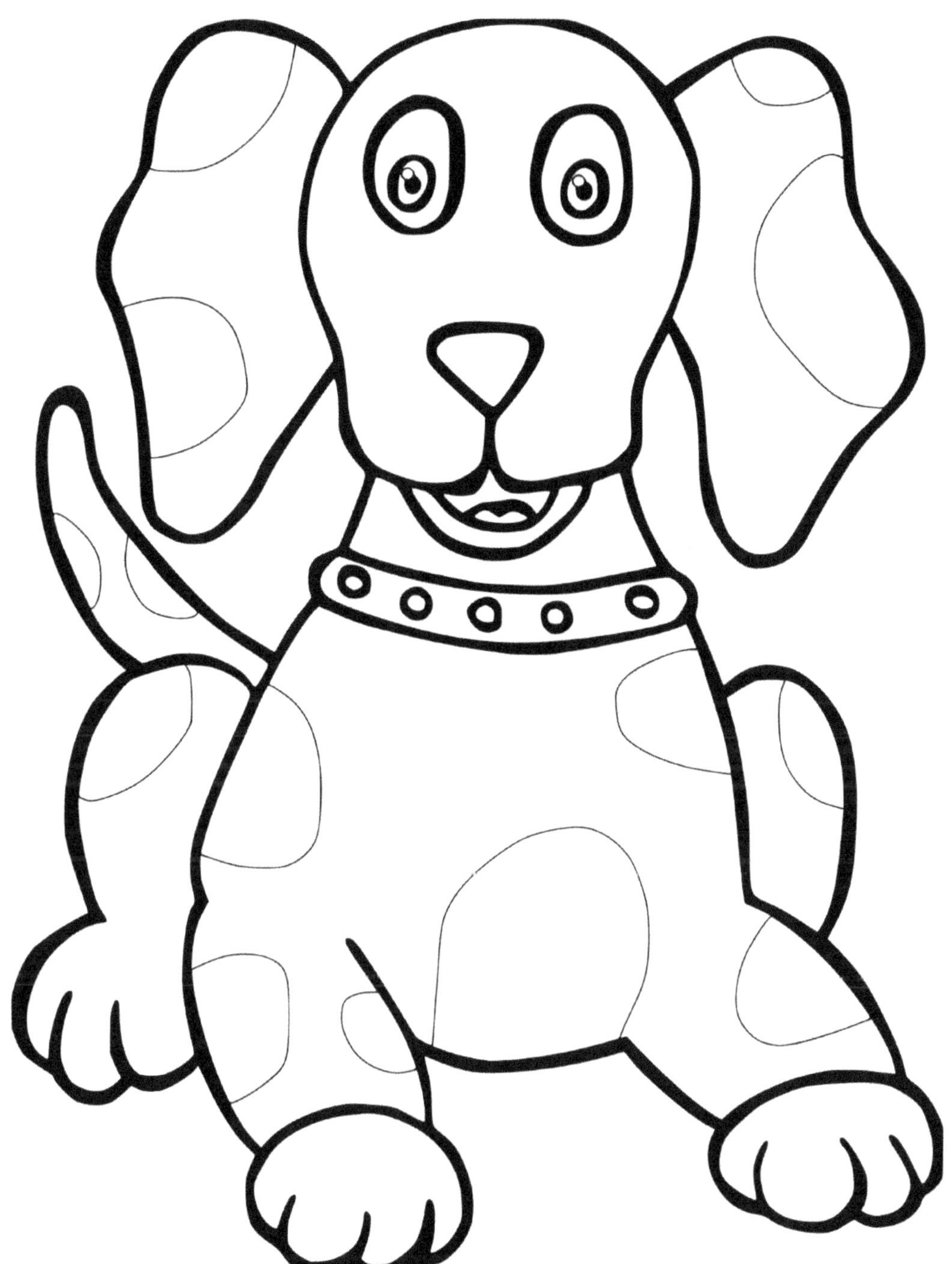

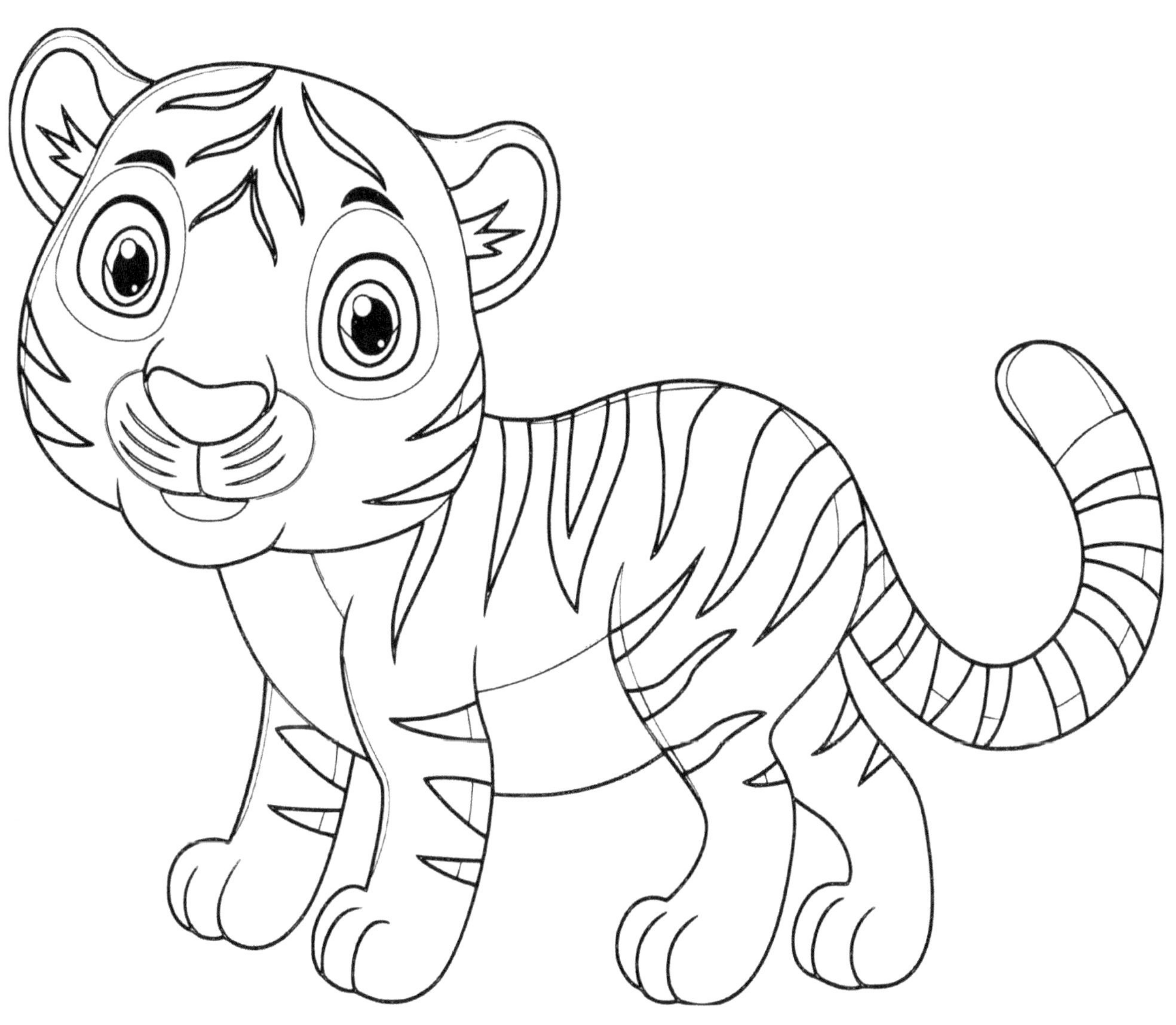

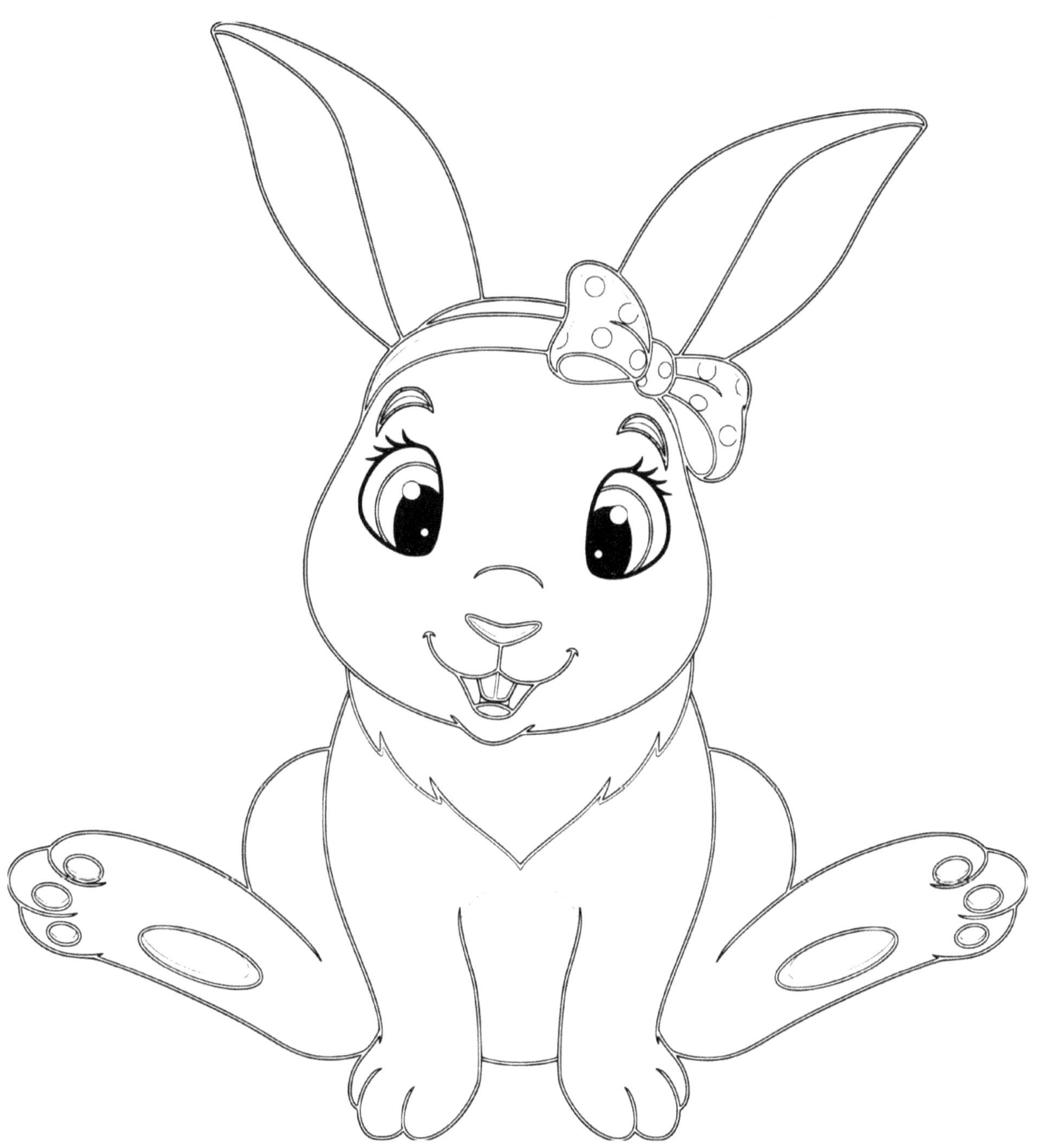

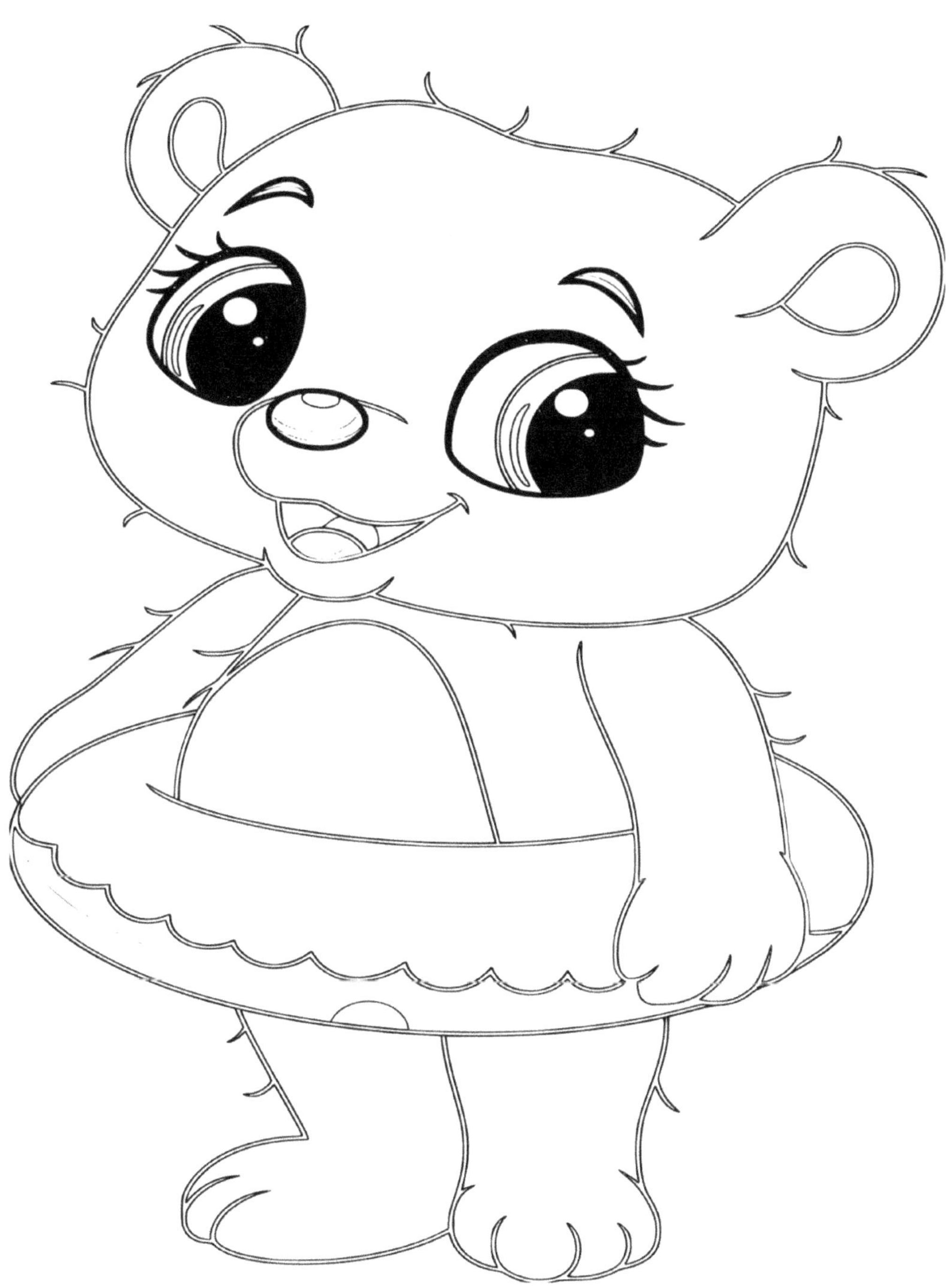

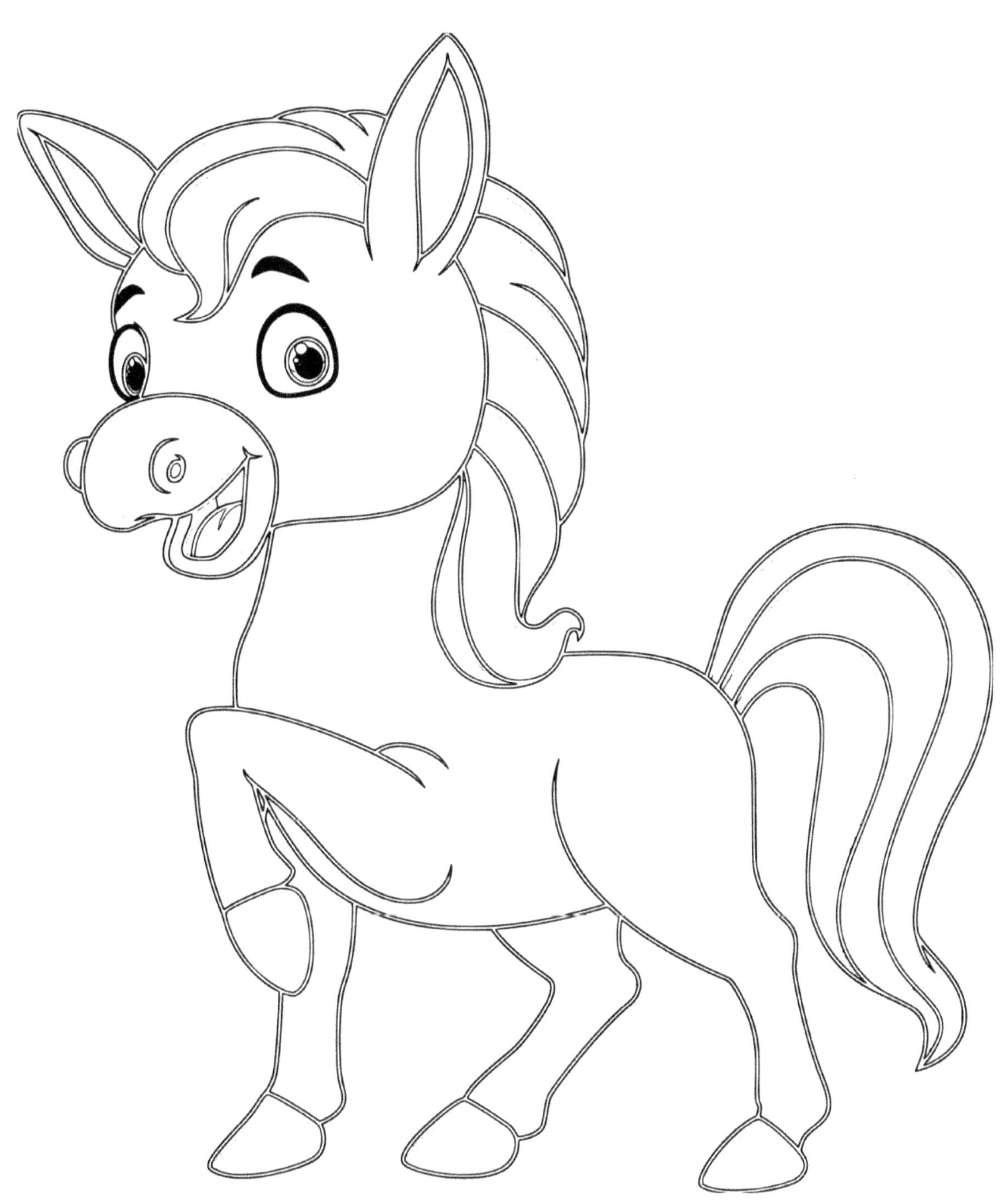

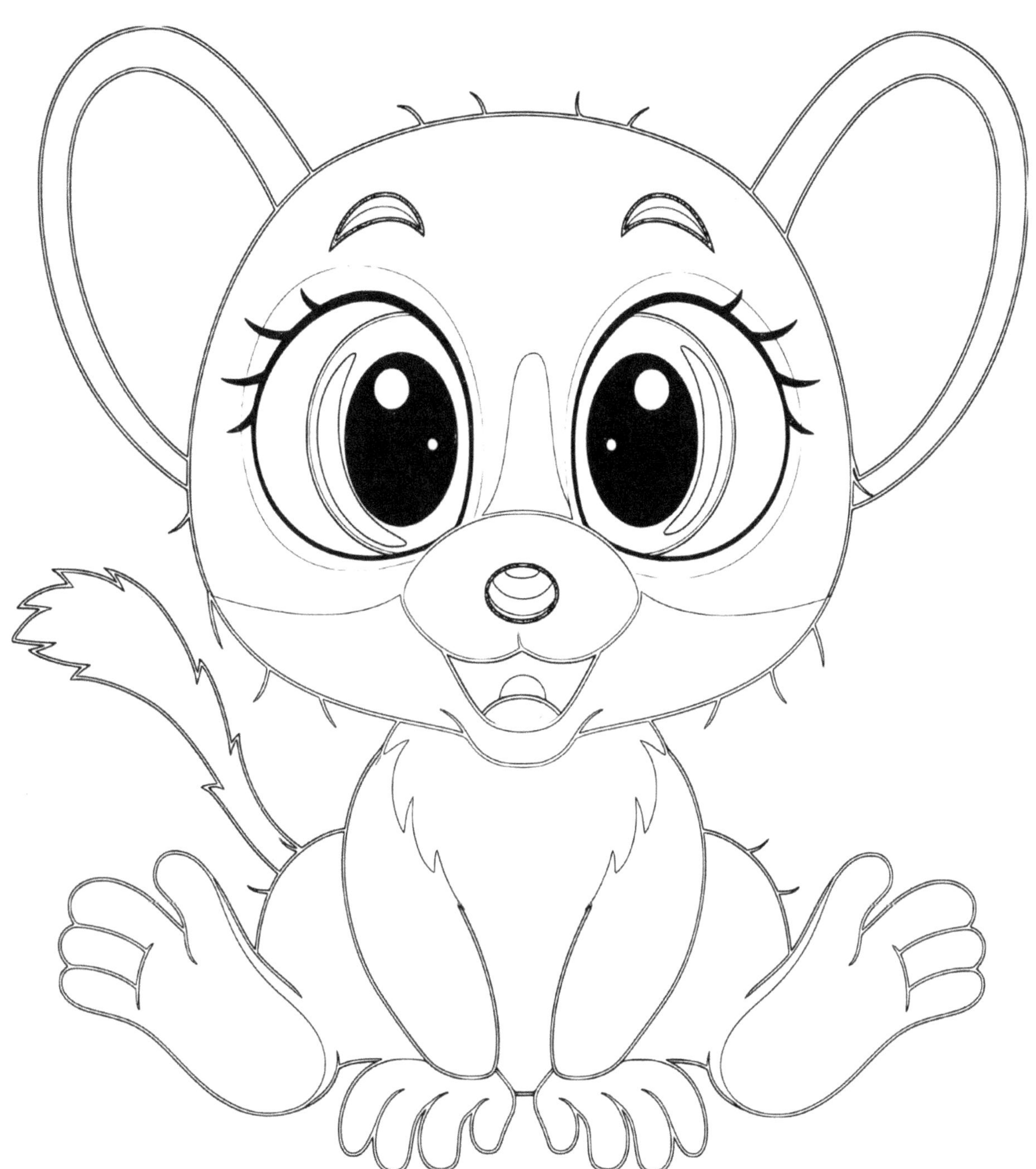

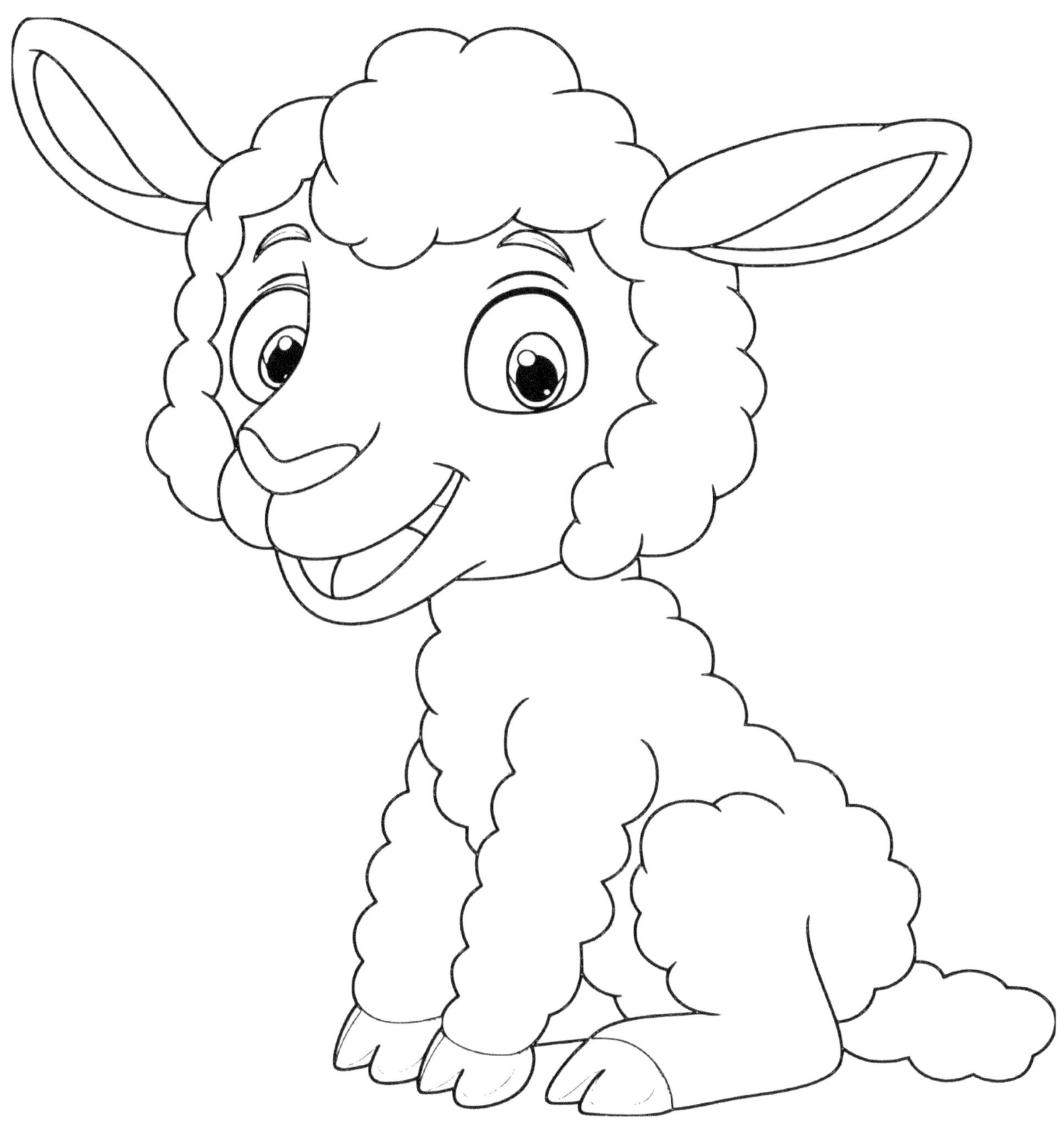

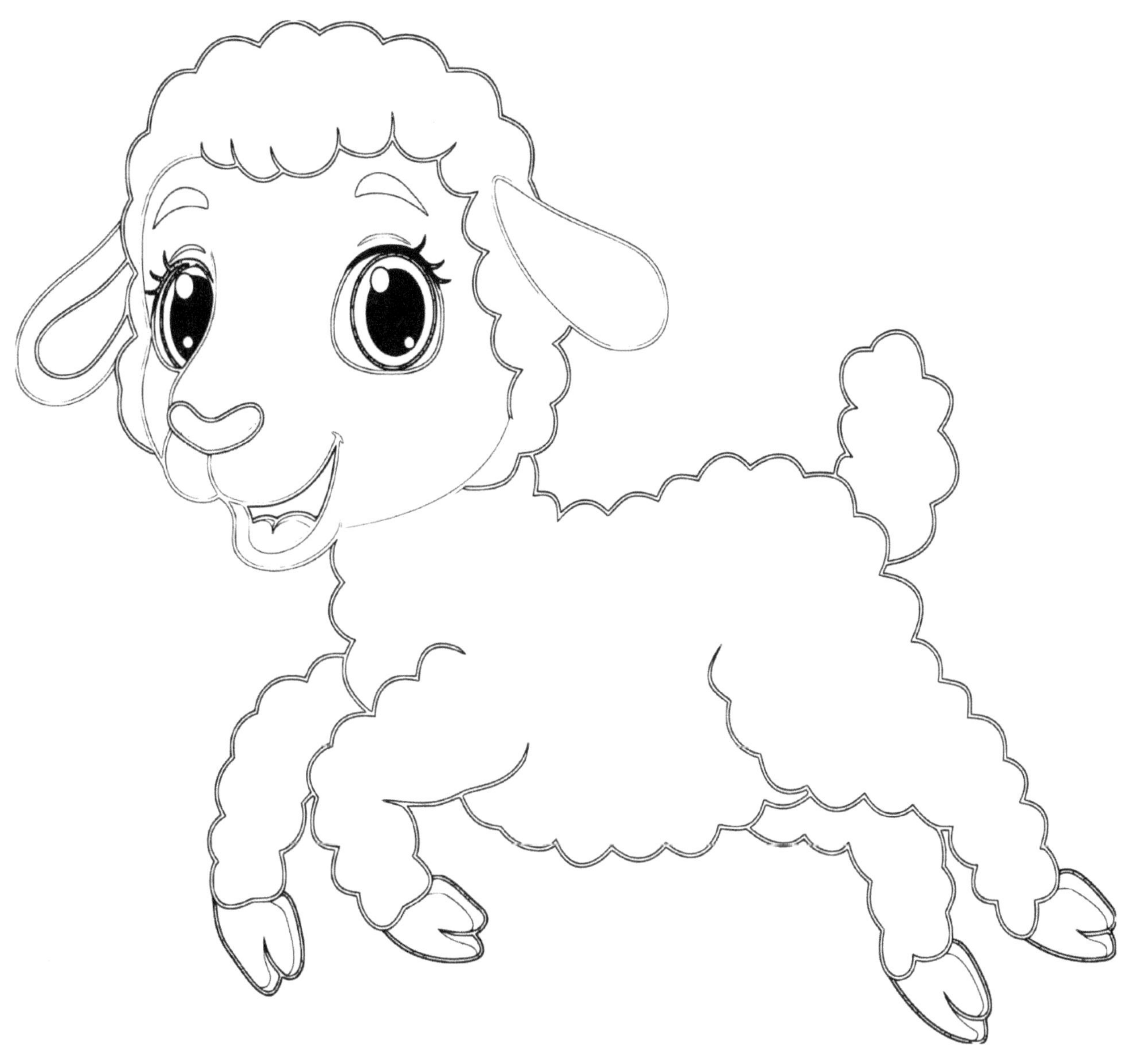

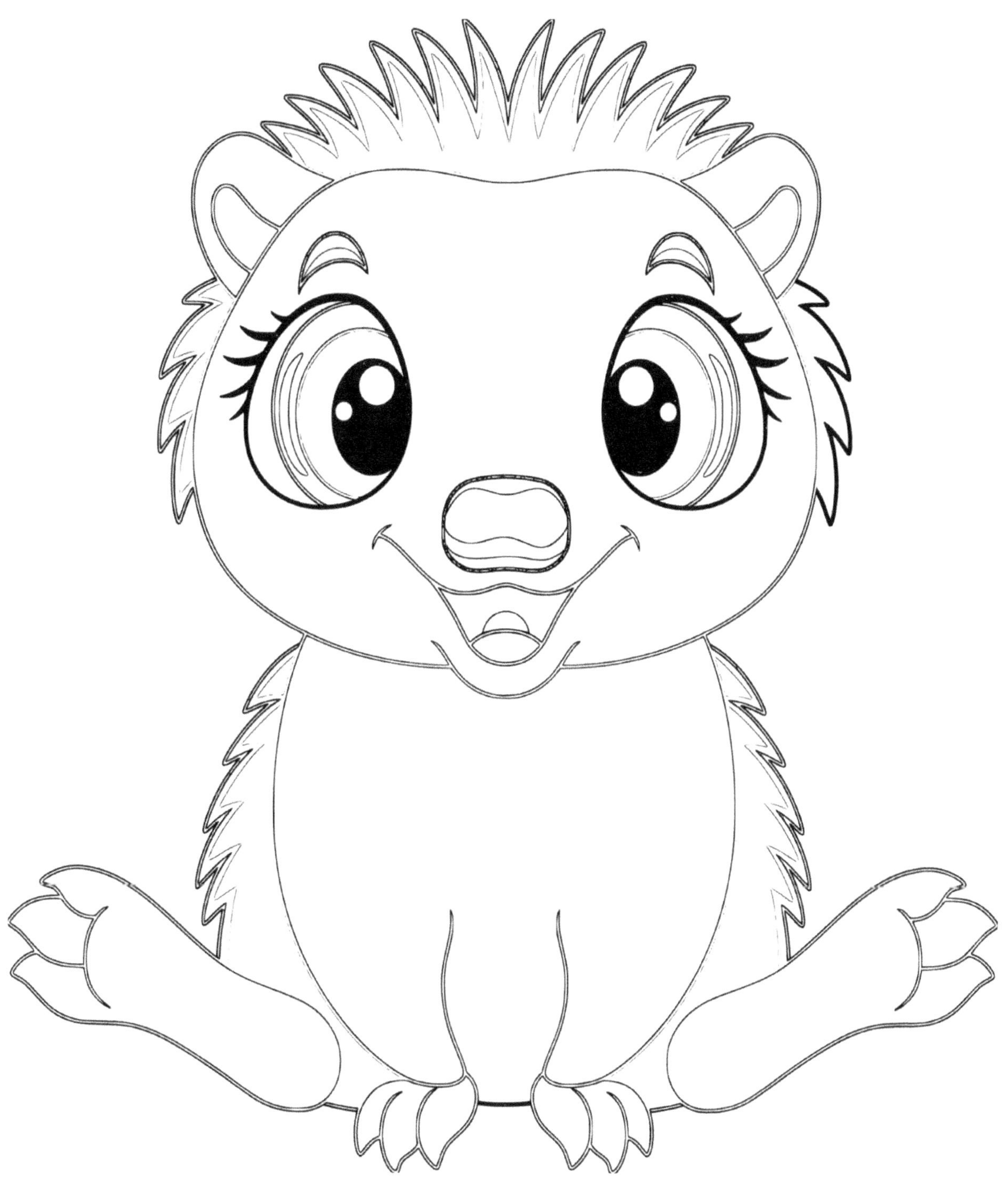

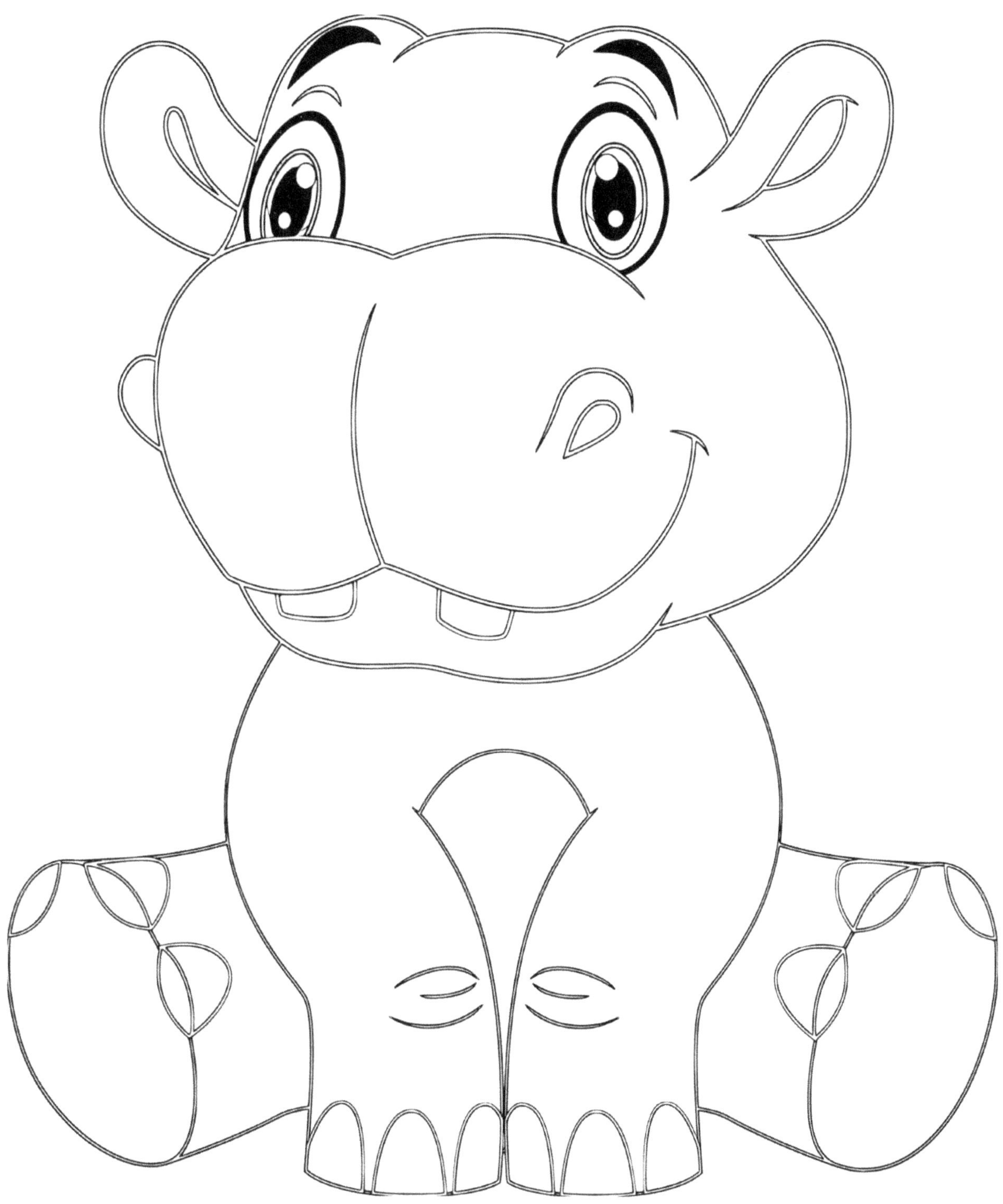

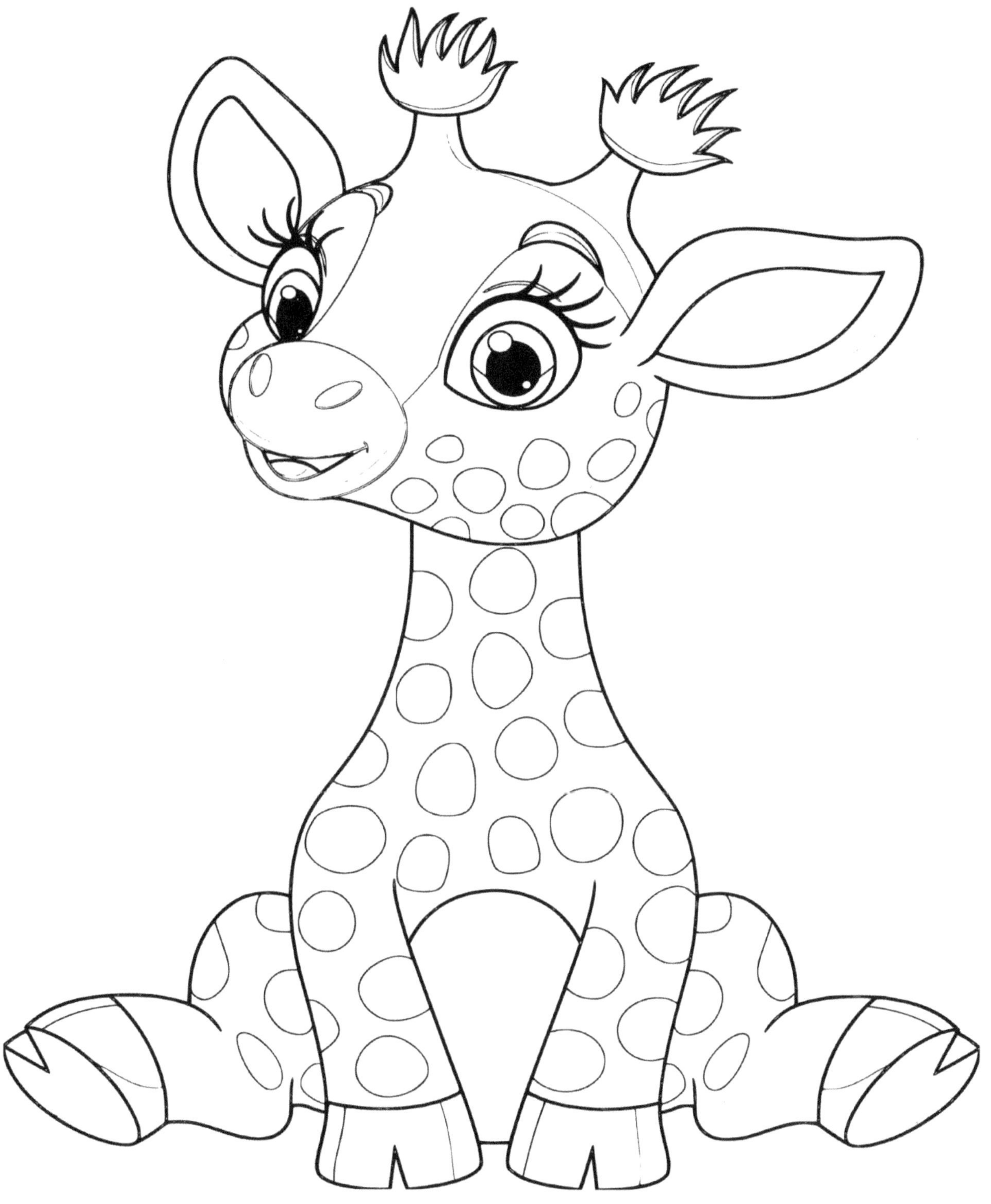

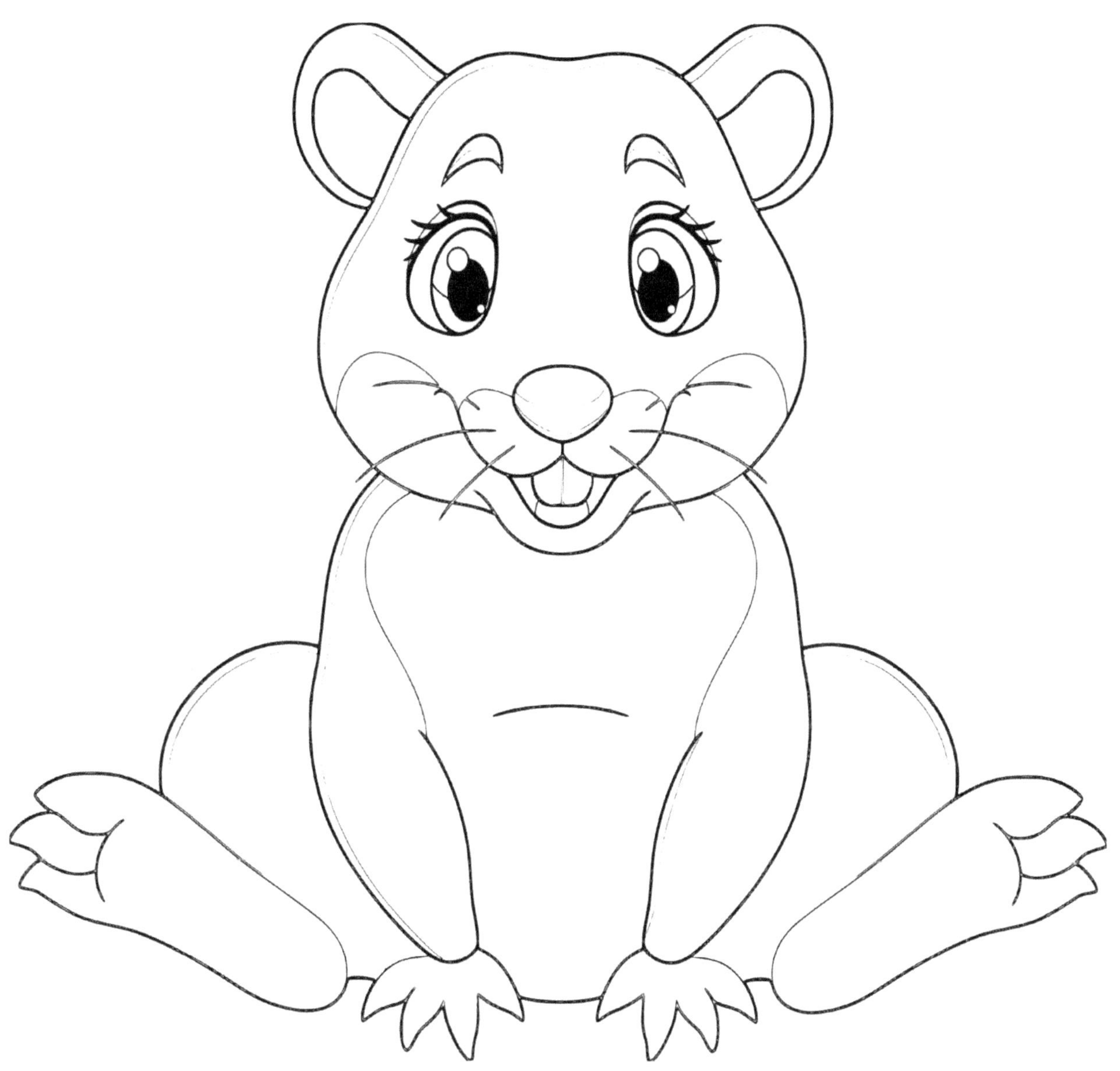

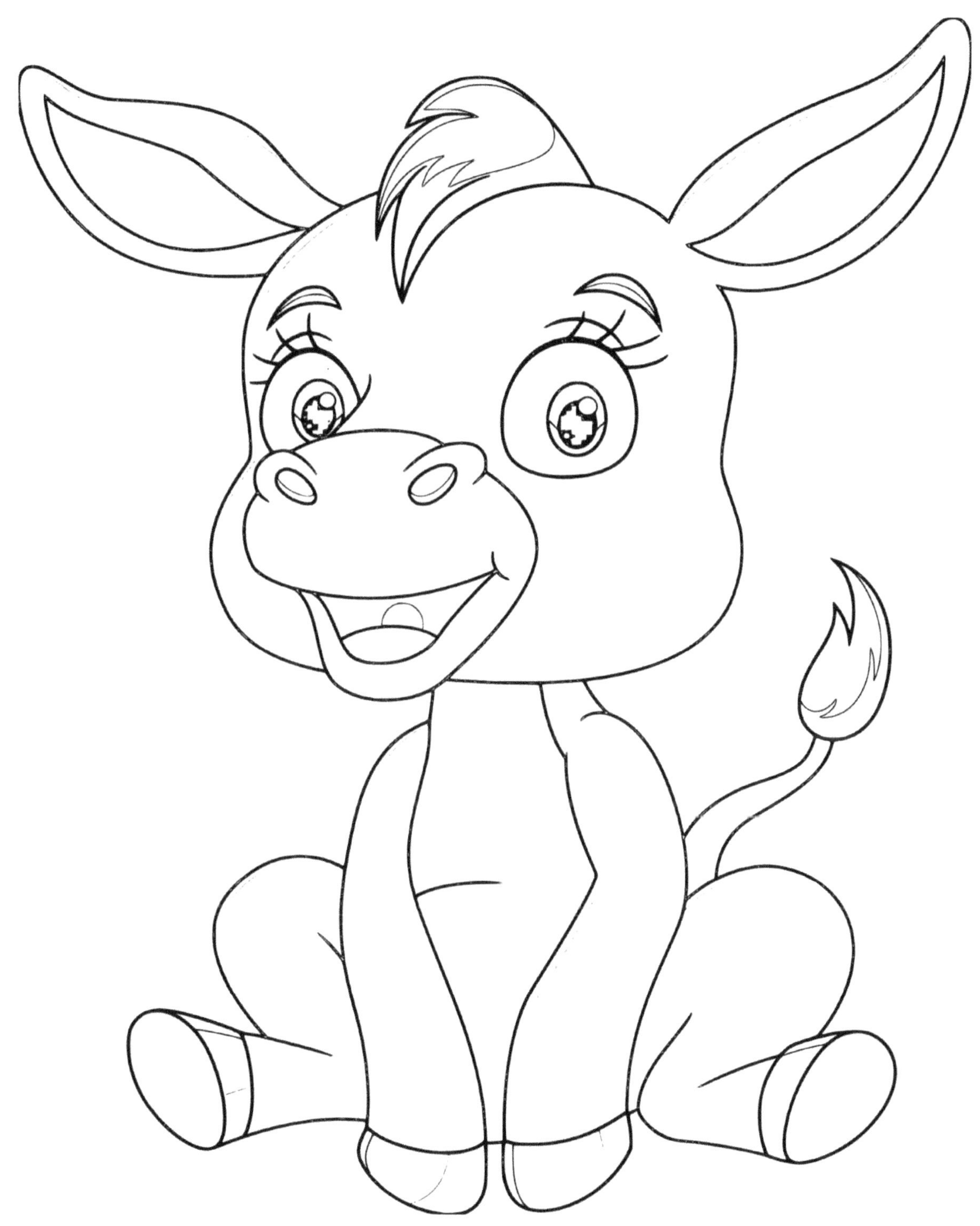

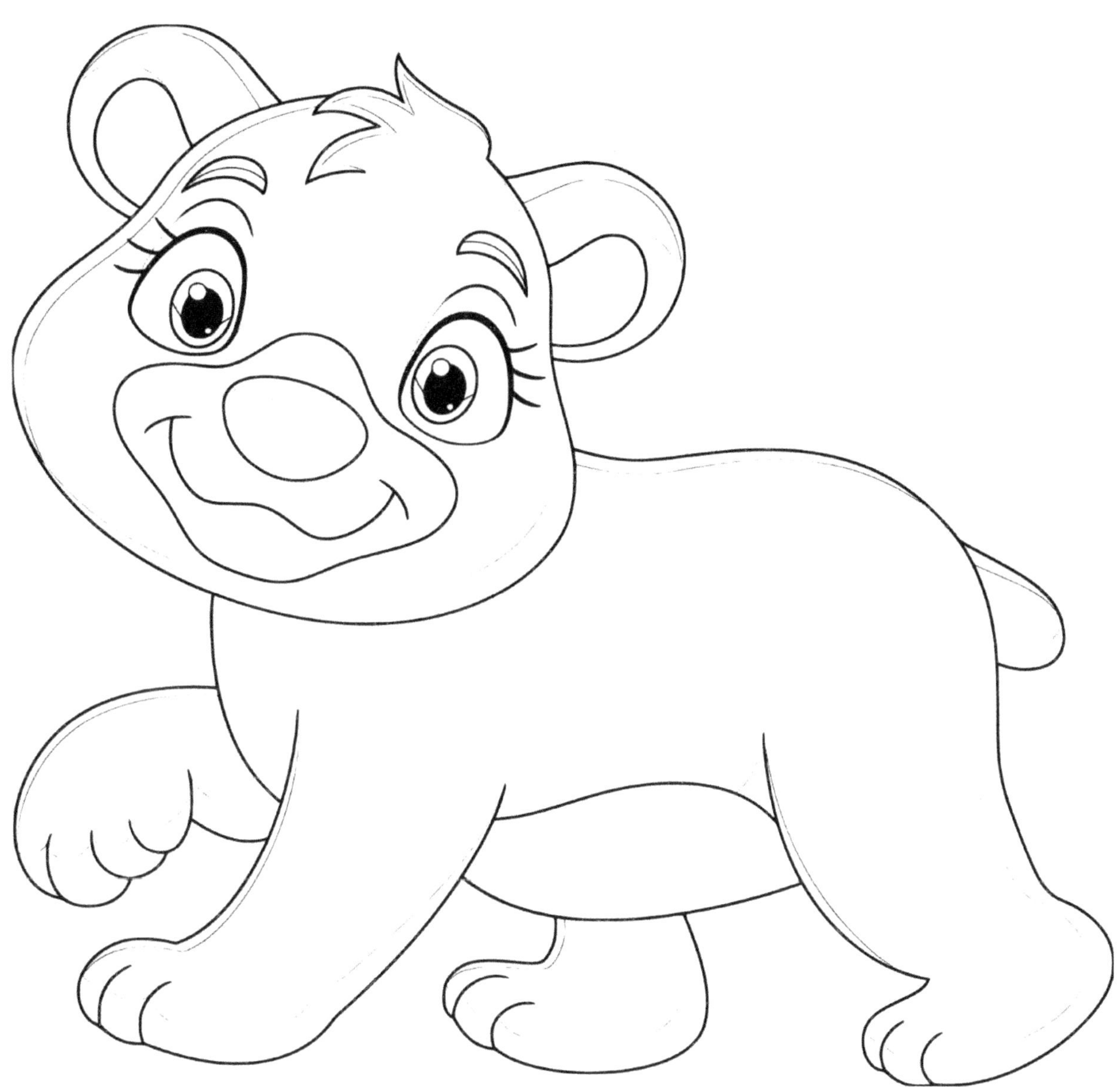

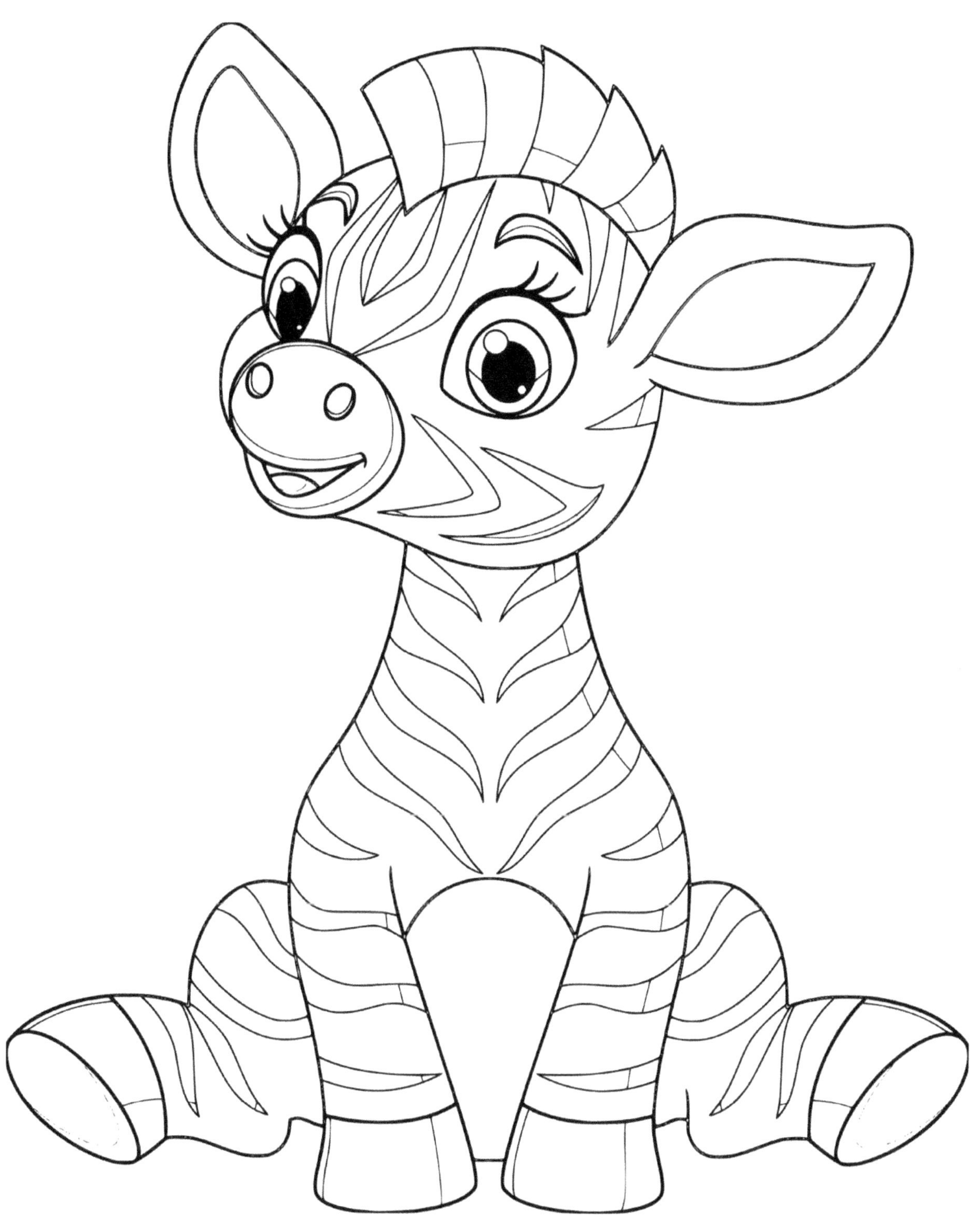

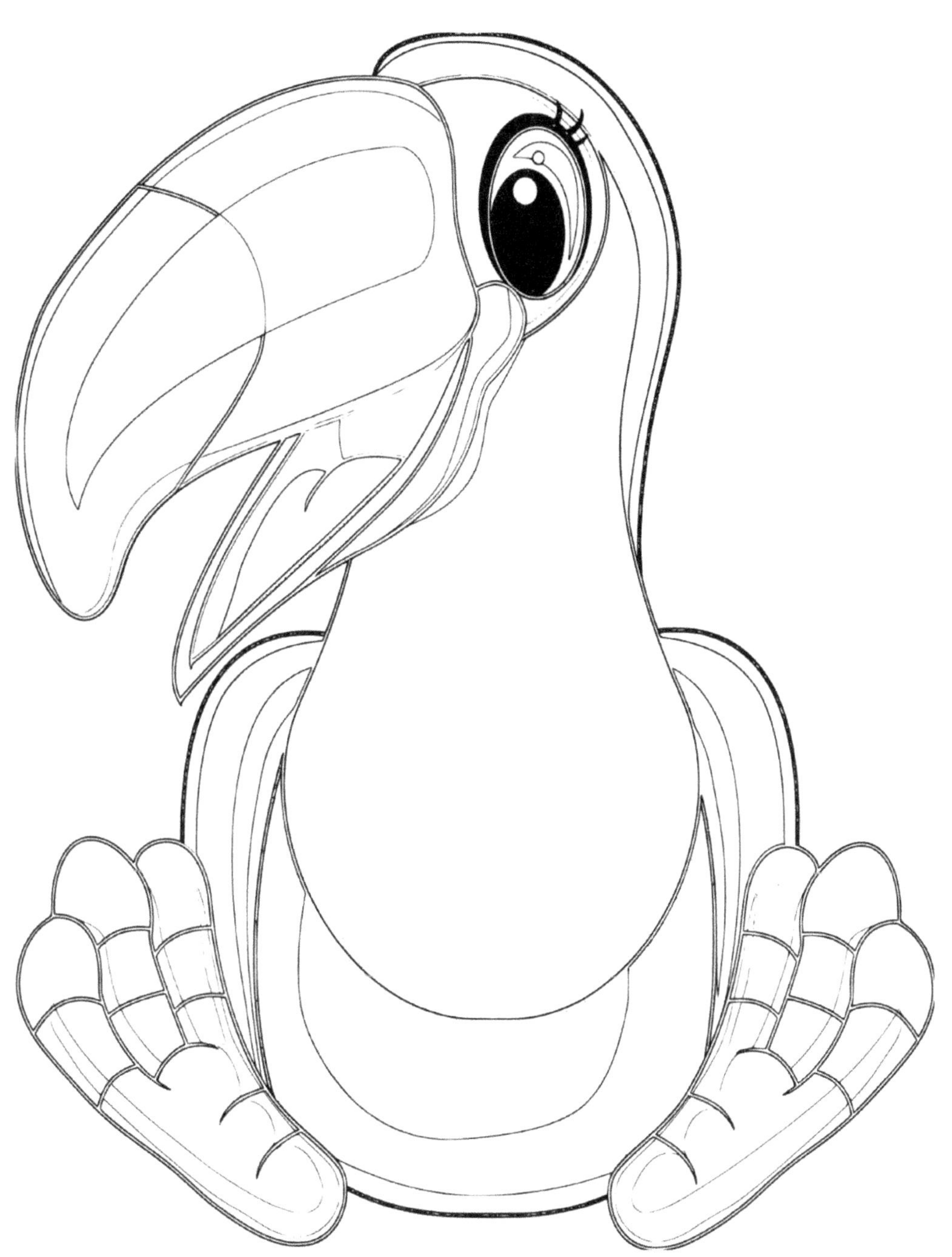

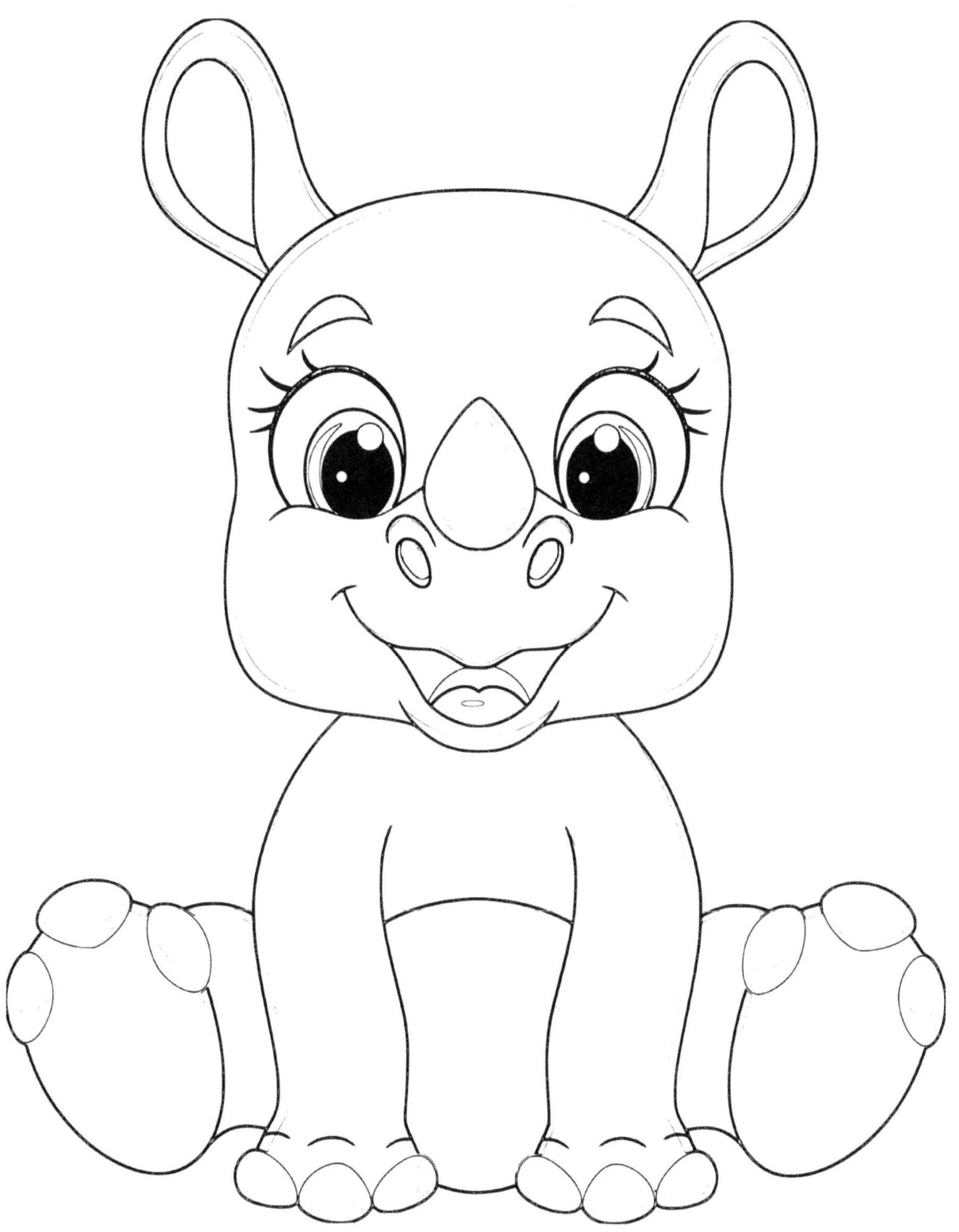

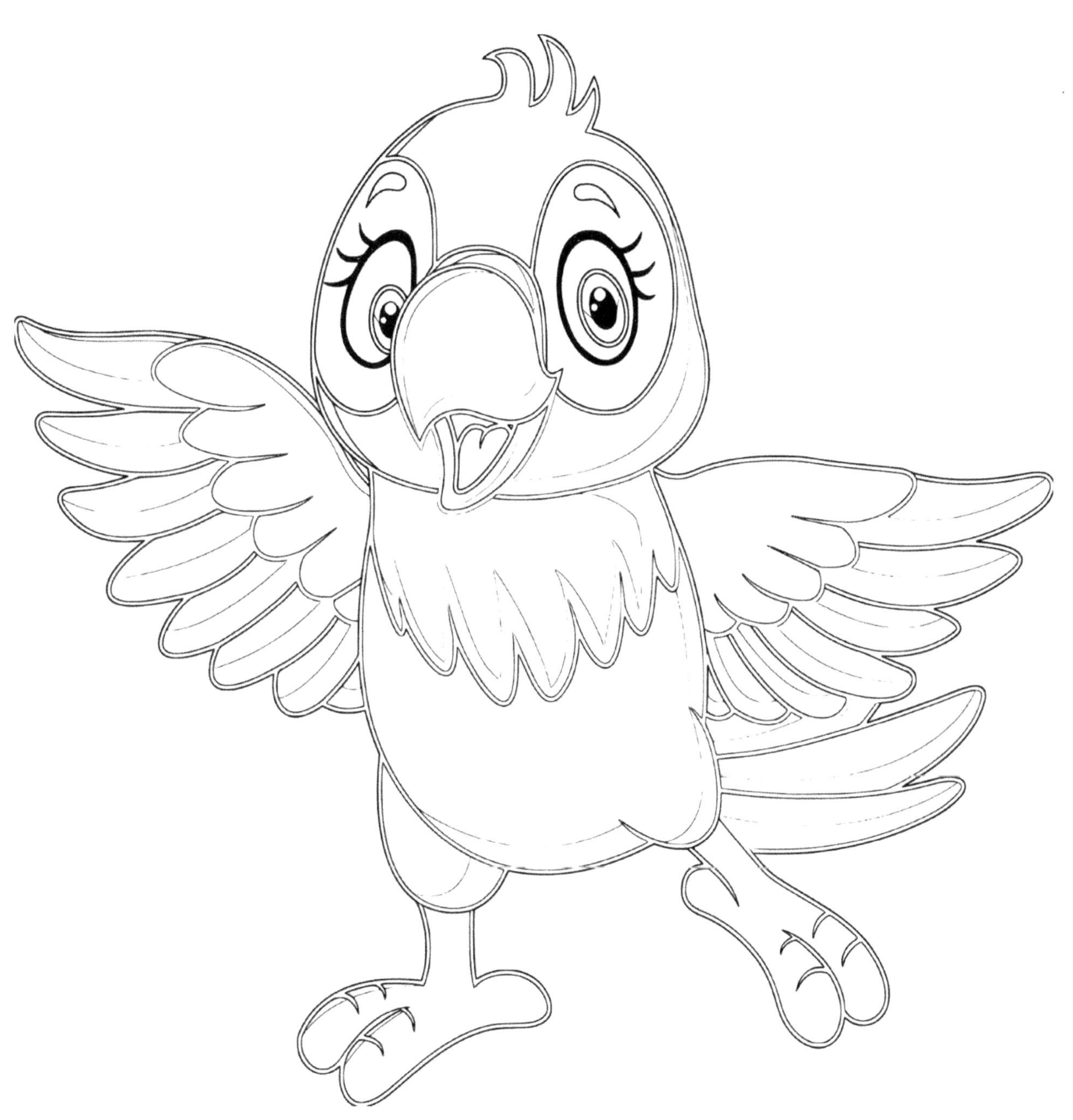

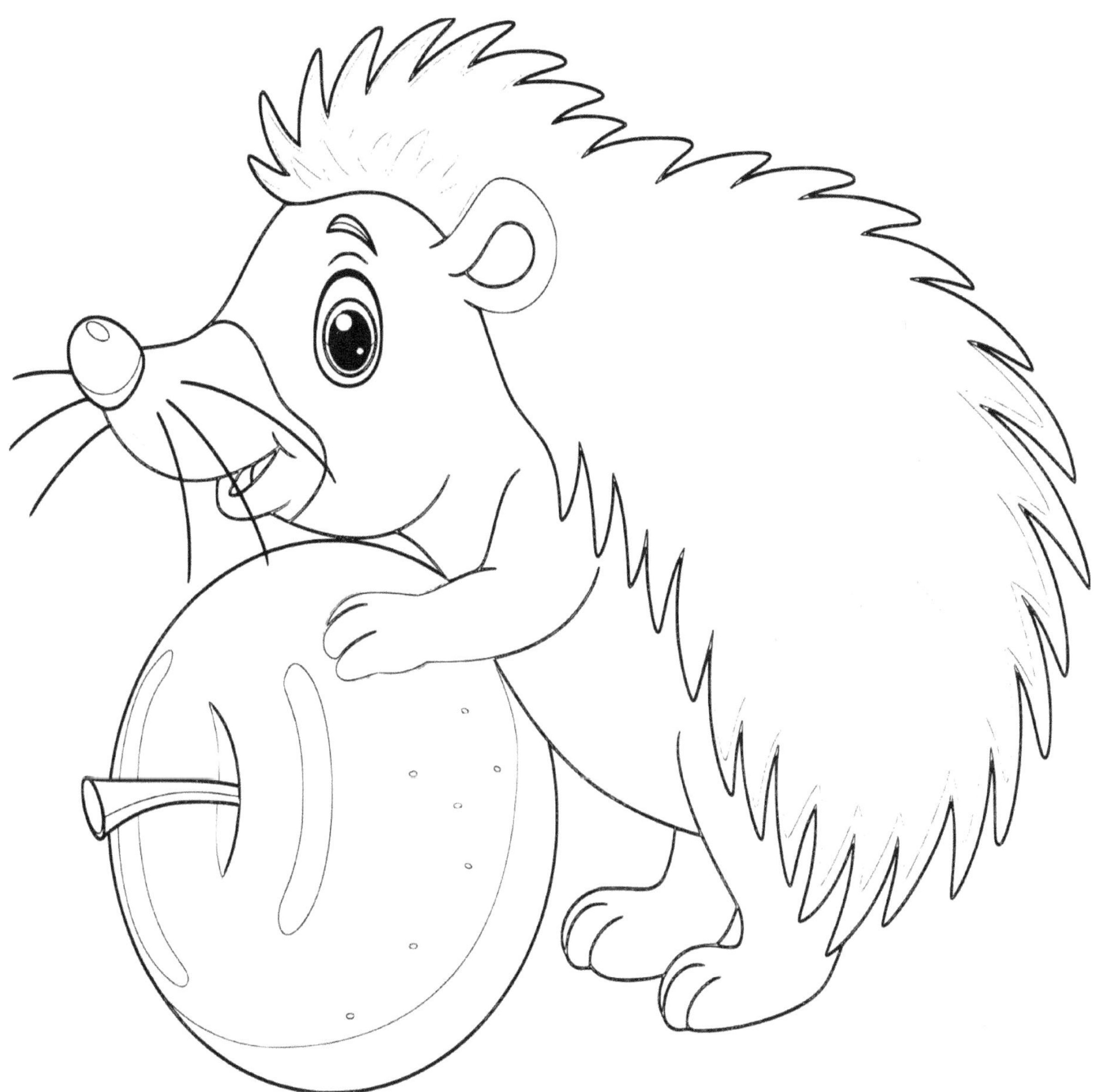

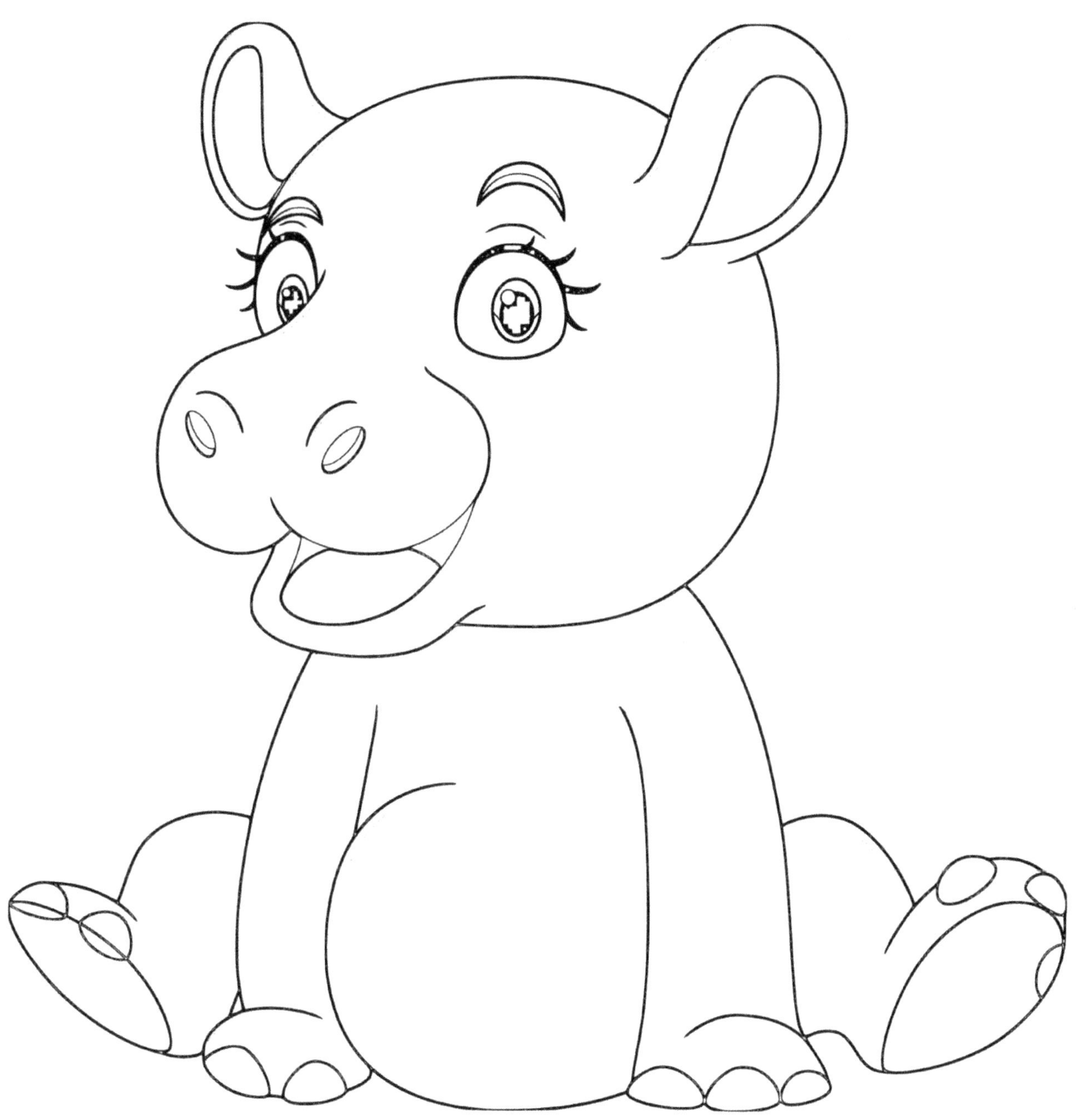

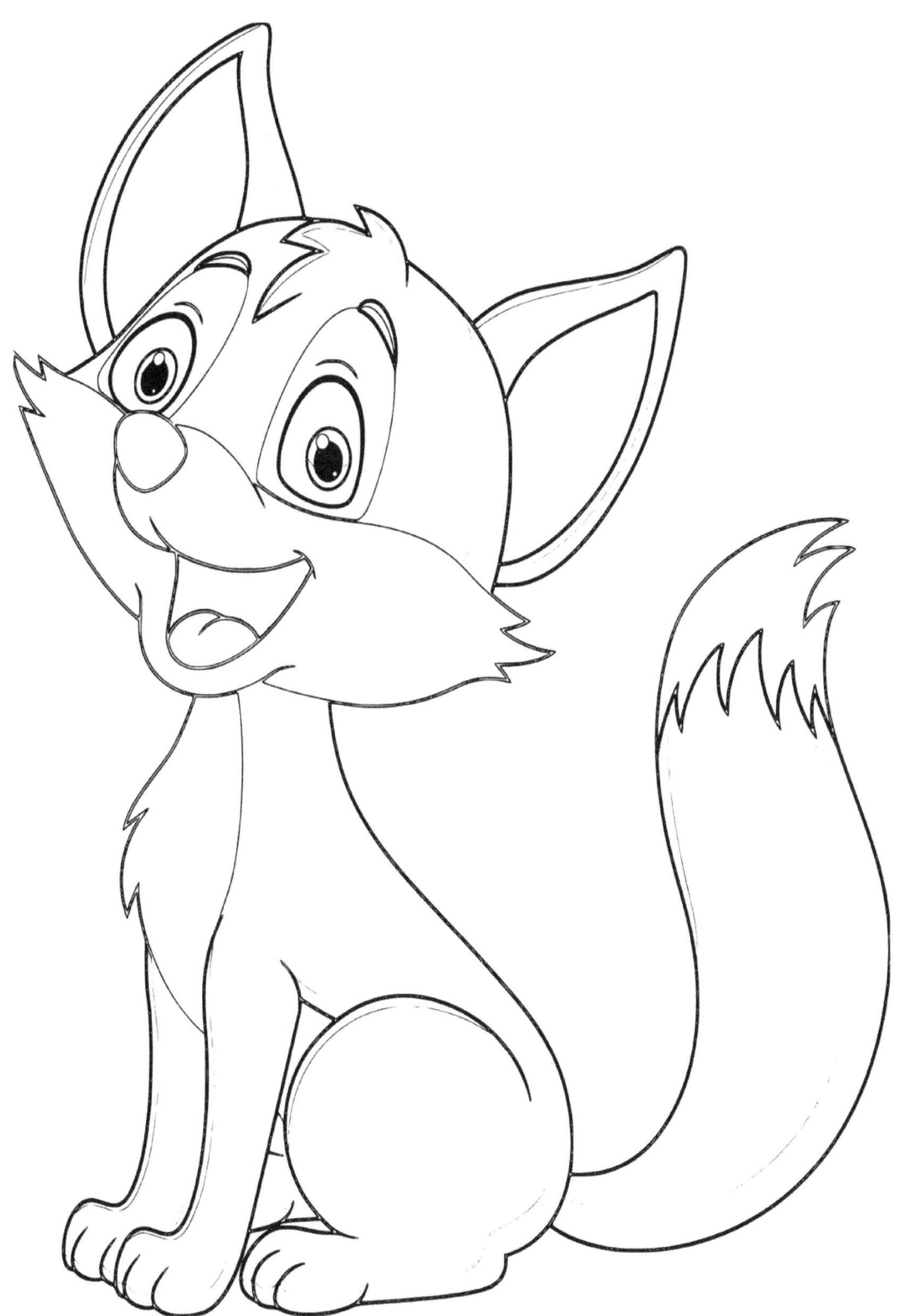

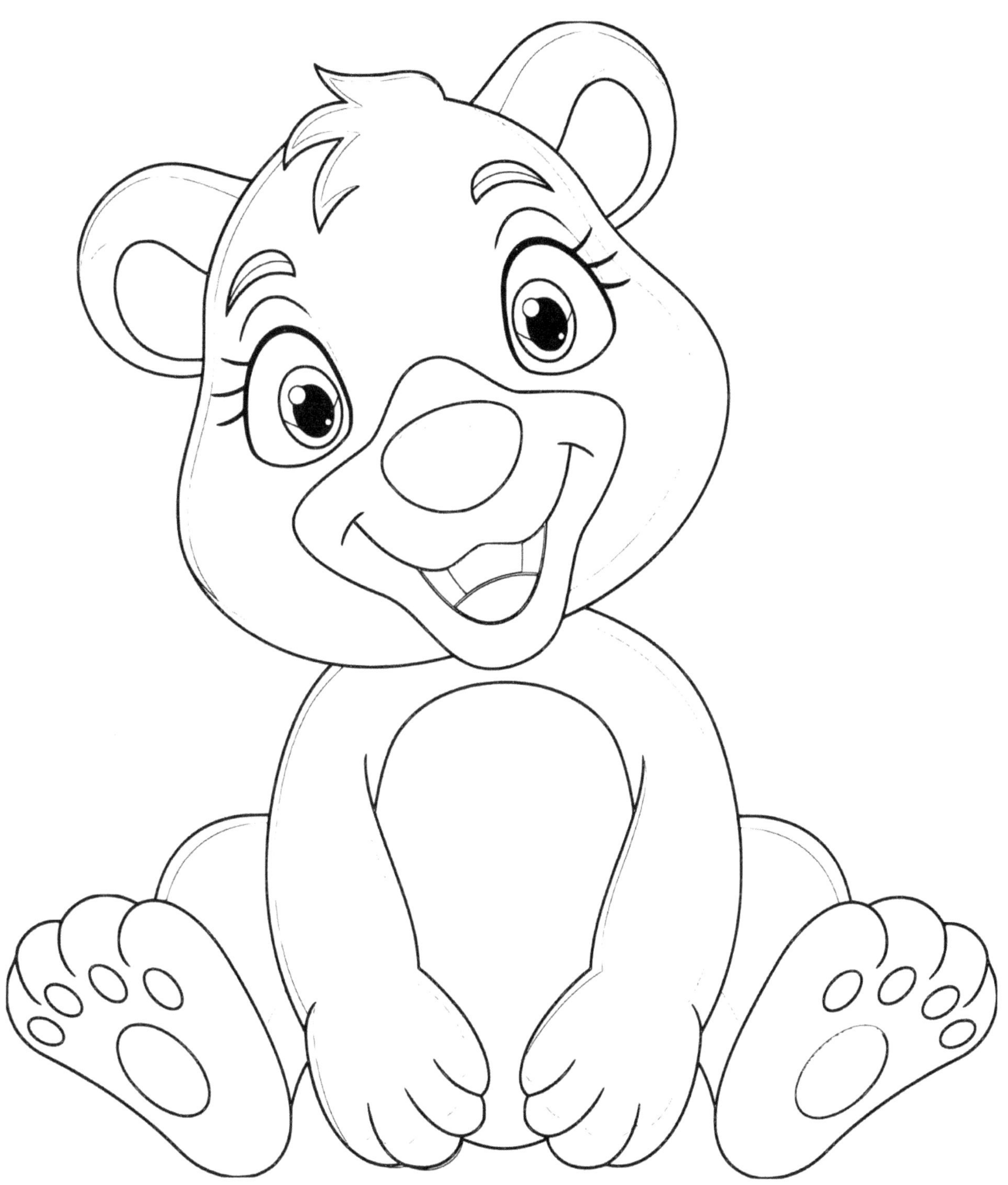

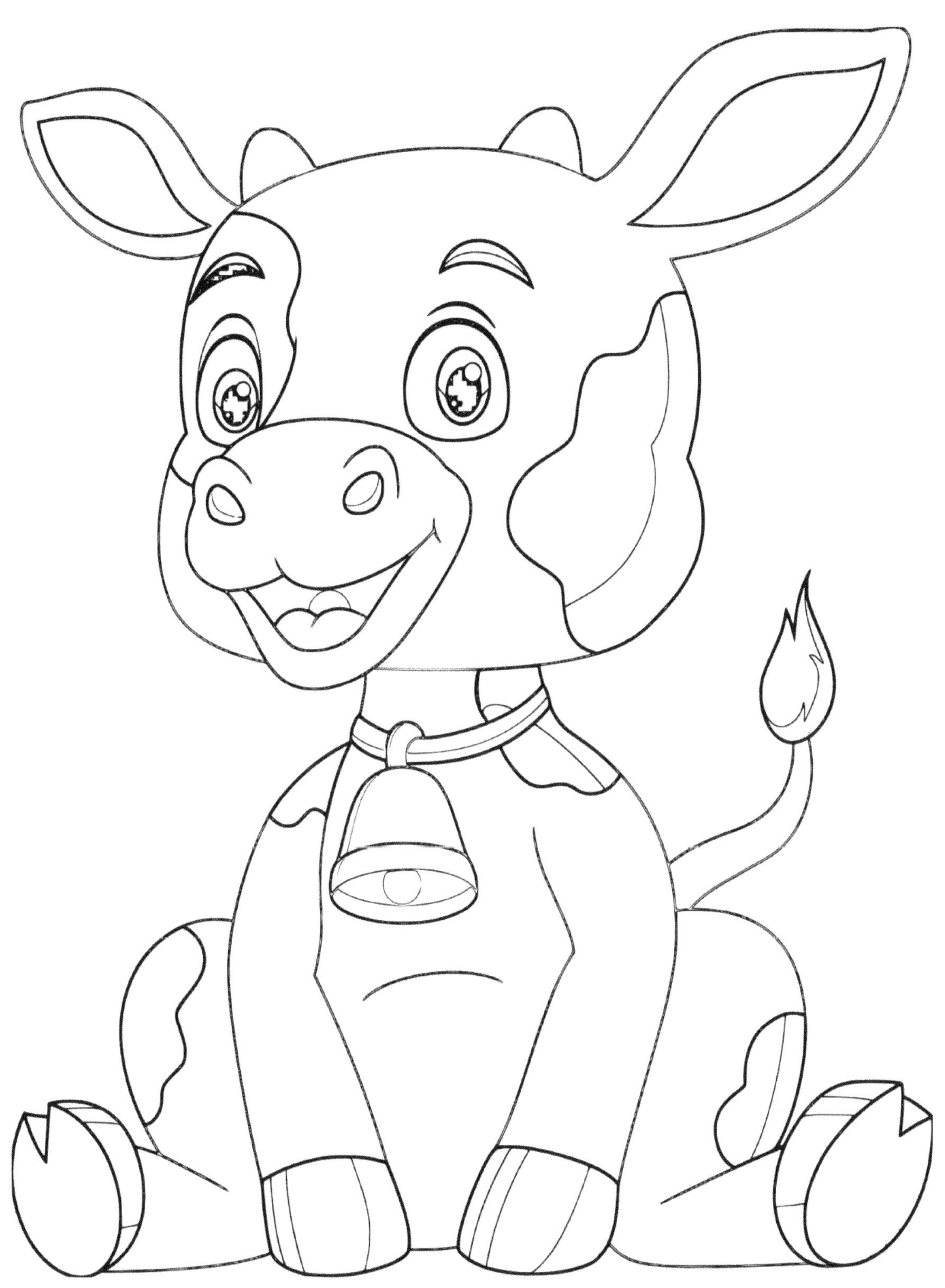

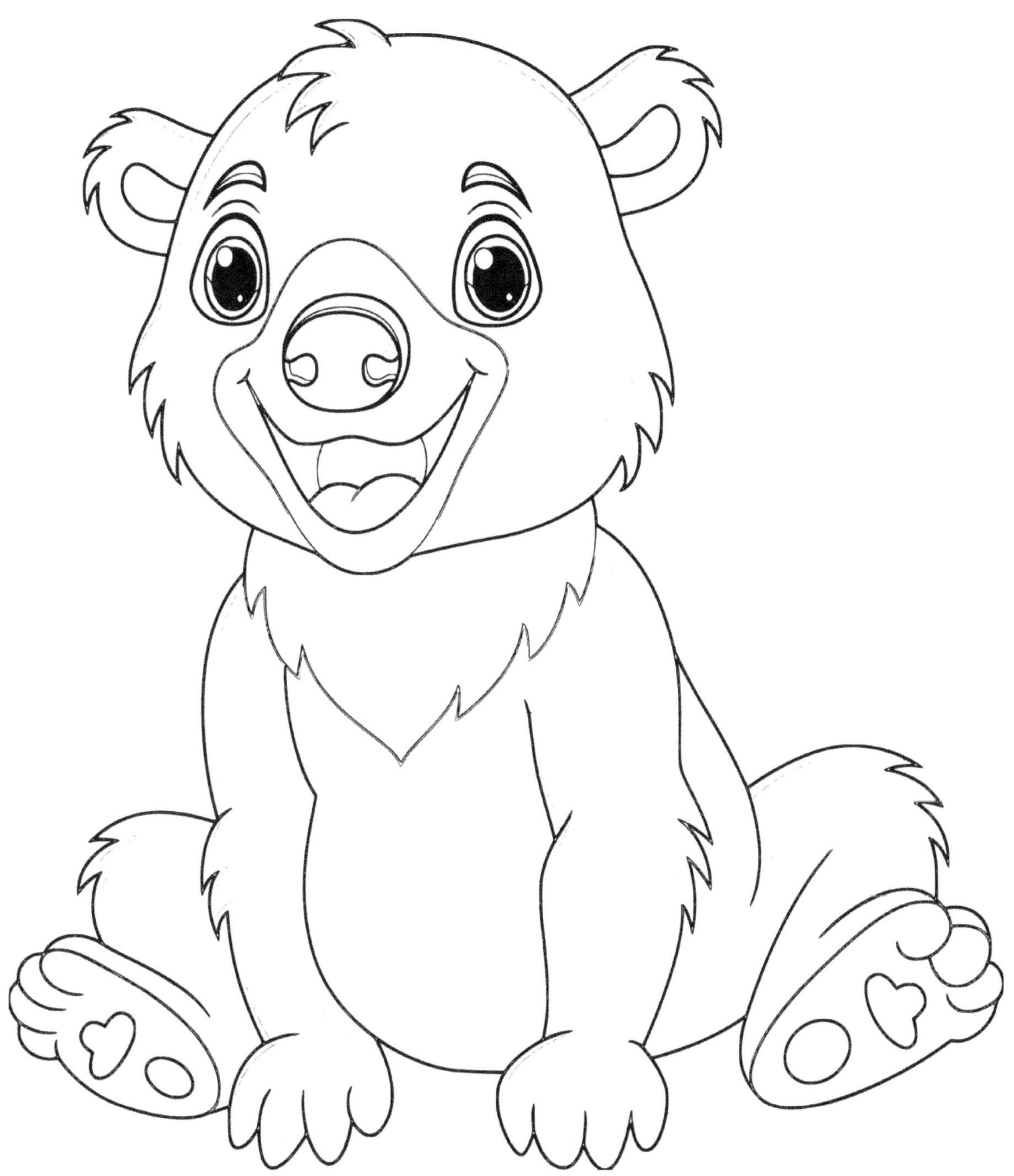

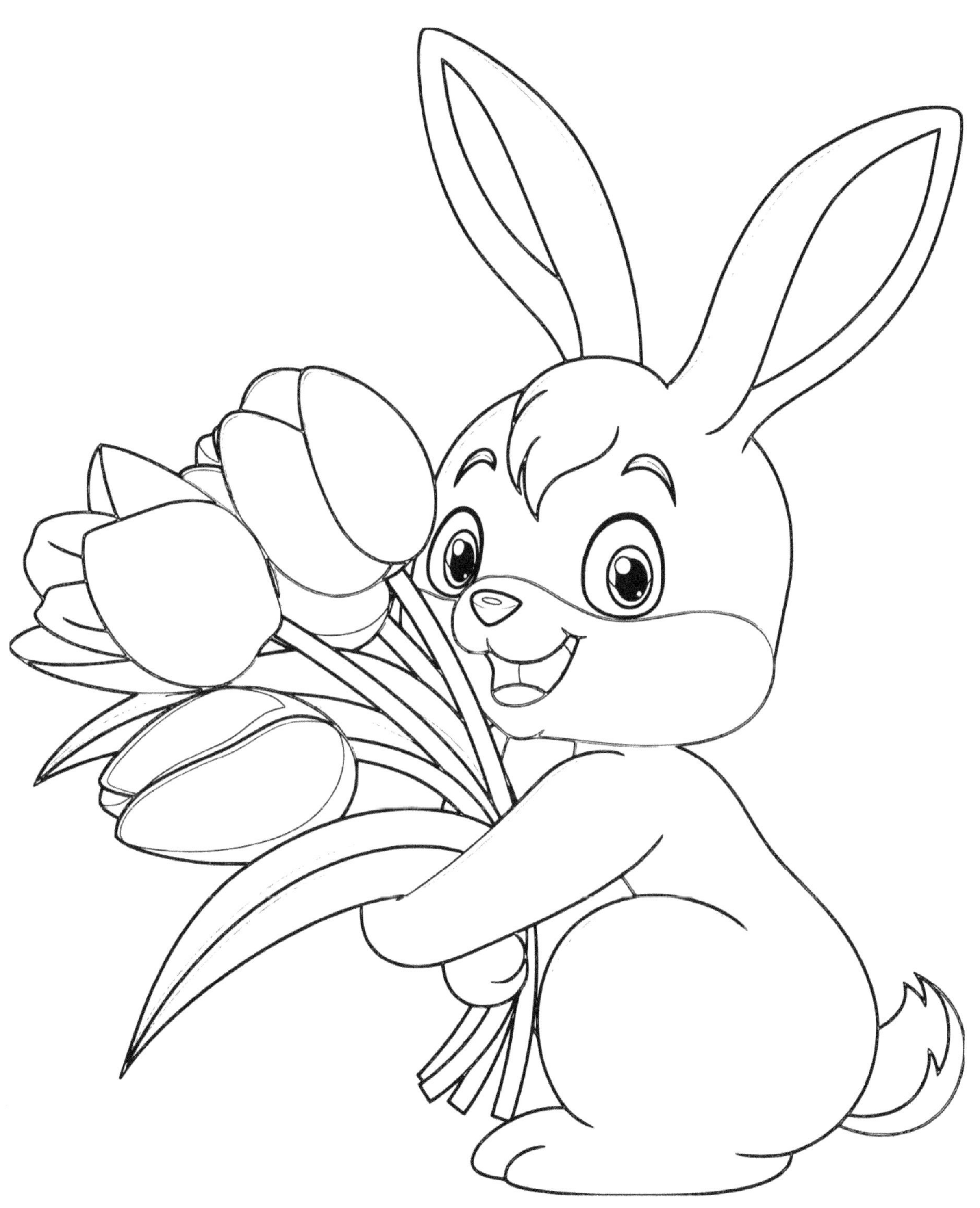

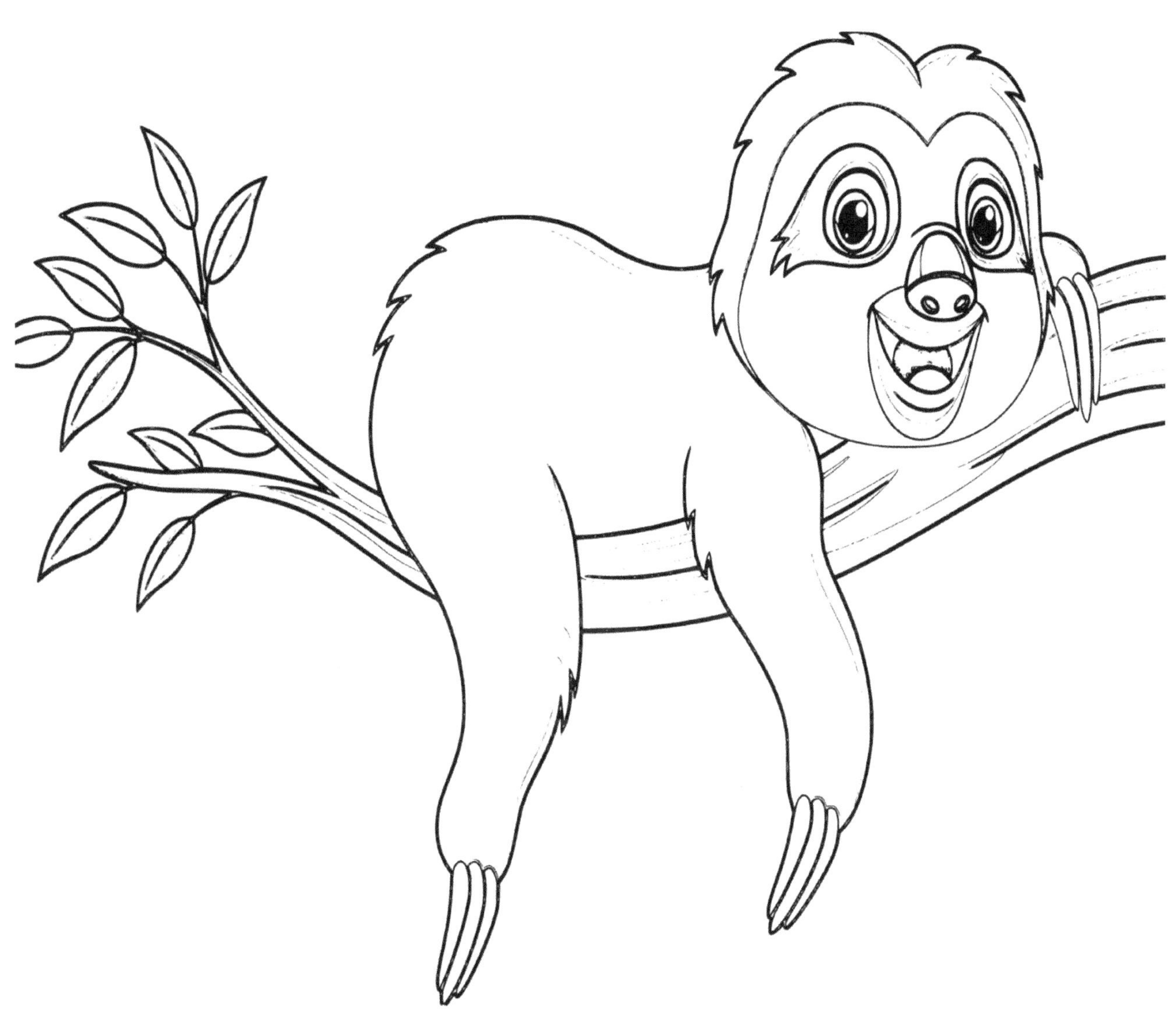

www.ingramcontent.com/pod-product-compliance
Lightning Source LLC
LaVergne TN
LVHW080044170826
845677LV00024B/1595
* 9 7 9 8 8 4 7 0 2 9 6 6 7 *